When Husbands Understand Their Assignment:
A Wife's Perspective
Featuring

A Husband's Prayer: Elder Rickey Brown

Dr. Tracie Green - Brown

Copyright © 2023 Dr. Tracie Green-Brown. All rights reserved.

Scripture quotations marked "NASB" are taken from the New American Standard Bible®, Copyright® 1960, 1962, 1963, 1971, 1972, 1973, 1975, 1977, 1995 by The Lockman Foundation. Used by permission. Scripture quotations taken from the Amplified® Bible (AMP), Copyright © 2015 by The Lockman Foundation. Used by permission. Scripture quotations marked "KJV" are taken from the Holy Bible, King James Version, Cambridge, 1769 Scripture quotations marked "NIV" are taken from Holy Bible, New International Version®. Copyright ® 1973, 1978, 1984 by International Bible Society. Used by permission of Zondervan Publishing House. Scripture quotations marked "NLT" are taken from the Holy Bible, New Living Translation, copyright 1996. Used by permission of Tyndale House Publishers, Inc., Wheaton, Illinois 60189. All rights reserved. Scripture quotations marked "TLB" or "The Living Bible" are taken from The Living Bible Kenneth N. Taylor. ®electronic ed. ® Wheaton: Tyndale House, 1997, c1971 by Tyndale House Publishers, Inc. Used by permission. All rights reserved. Scripture taken from *THE MESSAGE*. Copyright © 1993, 1994, 1995, 1996, 2000, 2001, 2002. Used by permission of NavPress Publishing Group. Taken from the Holy Bible: Easy-to-Read Version (ERV), International Edition © 2013, 2016 by Bible League International and used by permission.

DEDICATION

To my Sister-Girls.

To my single sisters, who want to know what they should expect from a potential husband.

To my married sisters, who might need to reevaluate their current situation.

There are certainly many other qualities a Godly husband should possess. I'm merely sharing a few that I feel are very important.

When Husbands Understand Their Assignment:
A Wife's Perspective

ACKNOWLEDGEMENTS

I would like to thank my husband, Elder Rickey Brown, for his constant love, support, and encouragement. You are the best! I love you so much.

I would like to thank my children, Carlos and Cherokee. I am so proud to be your mother. I pray you will be amazing husbands one day! I love you.

To my parents, Deacon Paul Green, Sr. and Mother Hattie Anderson-Green. They were the perfect role models.

TABLE OF CONTENTS

A Husband's Prayer: Elder Rickey Brown   ix

Introduction   1

Chapter 1   17
He is a Leader (He Allows God to Lead Him)

Chapter 2   28
He Loves His Wife as He Loves Himself

Chapter 3   39
He is a Provider

Chapter 4   46
He is a Protector

Chapter 5   55
He is a Supporter

Chapter 6   62
He is Loyal and Trustworthy

Chapter 7   71
He Only Has Eyes For You

Chapter 8   82
He Understands the Importance of Intimacy in a Marriage

Chapter 9   93

He Understands the Importance of Sex in a Marriage

Chapter 10   103

He is Grateful and Appreciates His Wife

Chapter 11   112

He Keeps No Record of any Wrongs (He is Forgiving)

Chapter 12   119

He Gives Time-Outs (He is Patient)

Chapter 13   127

He Knows His Wife

Chapter 14   137

What is Important to You is Important to Him

Chapter 15   144

He Continues to Pursue You

Dr. Green-Brown's Tidbits of Wisdom	*168*
About the Author	*173*
Book Description	*176*

A HUSBAND'S PRAYER
BY: ELDER RICKEY BROWN
∞

Heavenly Father,

I thank You for being who You are. You are a good God. There is none like You. I thank You for Your many blessings. I give You glory, for You are worthy to be praised!

Lord, I want to Thank You for the wonderful gift You gave me – MY BEAUTIFUL WIFE. Thank You for the privilege of having her by my side for over eight (8) years. She is the love of my life! Your Word reminds me that every good and perfect gift is from above. (James 1:17a) God, help me to always love and cherish my amazing gift.

I thank You for giving me a loving wife to share the rest of my life with. When I'd almost given up on finding a compatible mate, You allowed me to be in the right place, at the right time. That night, I saw a lovely lady, with a red flower in her hair from across the room. This lovely lady eventually became my wife. When I found her, I found a good thing! I will never take her for granted. Lord, help me to always love, honor, respect, provide, and protect her in the manner she deserves. Lord, You gave her to me and I am striving every day to keep her. Thank You for being the Head of my life. Thank You for teaching me how to be a good husband to my wife. Thank You for teaching me the importance of being very intentional when it involves my wife. I tell her and try to show her how much I love her every day. I pray that You will help her to fully understand exactly how deeply she is loved and valued. Besides You, God, she is the best thing that has ever happened to me! Thank You, Jesus!

I pray for our marriage. Sustain our union, God. Shield and protect us from the enemy who seeks to destroy marriages. I plead the Blood of Jesus over our marriage and marriages everywhere. Cancel the assignment of the enemy. Every plan, trick, scheme, or trap that Satan tries to set, Lord, let it fail. He will not succeed. For I know, Lord God, when we put You first in our lives, we will be victorious!

∞
"Therefore, what God has joined together,
let no one separate."
Matthew 19:6b (NIV)
∞

Lord, God, as my wife and I continue to pursue You, help us to be drawn into a deeper, and more intimate relationship with You. For we know that a personal relationship with you is the most important relationship to have.

∞
"For what profit is it to a man if he gains the whole
world, and loses his own soul?"
Matthew 16:26a (NKJV)

∞

Lord, help me to pursue my wife daily. I will continue to pursue her as if it is our very first date. I promise to always make her feel loved for the rest of her life. Help me to always love my wife, as You love the church.

In Jesus' name, Amen.

INTRODUCTION

Marriage is one of God's most wonderful gifts to mankind. Marriage is a blessing given to us by God to improve our lives and make life more enjoyable and fulfilling. It is a union worth working on, cherishing, and sustaining. Marriage is a union that God Himself instituted and blessed. The union between a husband and a wife is meant to be one of love, honor, trust, respect, and support. They were created to help and support each other. This concept is introduced in the book of Genesis 2:20-24, in the amazing story of the creation of Eve. Adam needed a companion, a suitable helper, yet one could not be found. God recognized that it was not good for man to be alone and made a helper for him out of his own rib. God caused the man to fall into a deep sleep; and while he was sleeping, He took one of the man's ribs and then closed up the place with flesh. Then, God made a woman from the rib He had taken out of the man. He brought her to the man. The man said, *"This is now bone of my bones and flesh of my flesh; she shall be called 'woman,' for she was taken out of man."* This woman becomes Adam's companion and wife, setting the original example of God's design for marriage. What a wonderful story! For this reason, a man leaves his father and mother, and is joined to his wife; and they become one flesh.

> **"But from the beginning of the creation, God made them male and female. For this cause shall a man leave his father and mother, and cleave to his wife;" Mark 10:6-7 (KJV)**

Merriam Webster defines marriage as the state of being united as spouses in a consensual and contractual relationship recognized by law. As Christians, we often view marriage as a Holy Covenant before God. Marriage is considered sacred in the sight of God. Marriage is the most serious commitment that two people can make to each other. It is often considered the basis for the family structure. Within the institution of marriage, families are created, and children are raised. Marriage is not a mere legal agreement; it is a lifelong commitment. Marriage symbolizes love, intimacy, companionship and commitment between a husband and wife. They have vowed to be devoted to each other for the rest of their lives. When you marry someone, you also promise with all of your heart, mind, and strength that you will love and cherish them for better or for worse, for richer or poorer, in sickness and health, as long as you live. Marriage is a covenant you made before God. You promised to be committed to each other through the ups and the downs. You made a promise to remain together through the good and the bad. (If your life is in danger, remaining together is not advised.)

Many women say "finding" a good husband is extremely difficult nowadays. I usually don't hesitate to correct them and let them know that they are going about it the wrong way. They are out of order. "The husband is supposed to find you!"

"Whoso findeth a wife findeth a good thing, and obtaineth favour of the Lord." Proverbs 18:22 (KJV)

I must pause to mention this: Ladies, please don't be 'outside and in these streets' searching for a man. Pray and ask God to send you a husband and be patient. Put God first and continue to live your life. Use this time to develop a closer relationship with God. Use this time to focus on yourself and becoming the woman God wants you to be. While you are living a Godly life and waiting on God, you are actually already advertising for a Godly husband. (Ladies, remember that "men initiate" and we "respond.") In God's timing, he will find you. Oftentimes, God will send your husband directly to you. He will likely approach you and shoot his shot and if you're interested, you will respond accordingly and the rest will be history. **I'm on my soapbox.**

The inability to have a good husband or marriage can be attributed to the high divorce rate in America. Many divorces are due to infidelity, physical, mental, and emotional abuse, substance abuse, sexual incompatibility, and money. I can truly understand the caution many women have for delaying marriage. Marriage is a lifetime commitment. Well, at least, it is supposed to be a lifetime commitment. *"...To have and to hold from this day forward, for better, for worse, for richer, for poorer, in sickness and in health, to love and to cherish, till death do us part."* Marriage is romantic and exciting for many, but it's also a decision that will definitely change the rest of your life. For example, while many women may be ready for a commitment, there are many men who are not quite ready to take the plunge. He might not want a serious relationship or even marriage. Many men have a fear of commitment. Labels can frighten some men. Ladies, if you are in a relationship and you know that your mate isn't ready for marriage, you have an important decision to make. Why are you wasting your time? You know the relationship isn't going anywhere. If he's not ready for marriage, you can't force him to get ready. He certainly wouldn't be receiving any marriage benefits either, if you know what I mean; make him pay for the milk. If your mate is still wandering in the past, don't do it. If he has one foot in, and the other foot out of the relationship, don't do it. If he's thinking about what he will be missing once he settles down, and you are privy to the doubts that he's having about marriage, don't shrug it off. Don't pretend like everything is great or convince yourself that it's all in your head. You want this so bad, therefore, you look the other way. This is crucial. Snap out of it and pay attention. He is likely not ready for a commitment.

Ladies, be certain that you want to get married for the right reasons. If you're getting married because all of your friends are married, that's not a good enough reason to do it. Marriage is serious and shouldn't be taken lightly. If you're not ready to commit to one man or you're not willing to compromise, take time to consider your motive for getting married, as well. You should never get married out of guilt, or fear that this will be your last opportunity, with thoughts such as, *"I'm getting old, and my clock is ticking."* If your intuition tells you something is not right, definitely listen to your inner voice. You don't want to be in a marriage where you or your spouse isn't fully committed. The most successful marriages are often those where both partners are totally committed to making it work and making each other happy.

When I think of the qualities to look for in a husband, there are several that come to mind. There are many qualities every woman should look for in a potential spouse. Some of the qualities include:

- God-Fearing
- Loving
- Respectful
- Leader
- Honest
- Faithful
- Trustworthy
- Compassionate
- Loyal
- Dependable
- Supportive
- Protector
- Provider

- Great Communicator
- Sense of Humor

If you are a single woman and you desire to be married, ask God to send you a compatible mate. When praying for a husband, you want to be very specific. If you have certain qualities and expectations in a spouse, you should definitely pray and ask God for what you want. Make your requests known unto God. Tell God exactly what you desire in a mate.

"Be careful for nothing; but in everything by prayer and supplication with thanksgiving let your requests be made known unto God."
Philippians 4:6 (KJV)

The wonderful qualities that we look for in a husband are very important to us. The qualities listed are very significant. He might not possess all of the qualities listed, however, he should at least possess the majority of them. I'm just saying! During the early stage of your relationship, you should pay close attention to your partner. Take time to get to know him. I've even heard the seasoned church mothers and missionaries say to "study" him. Don't be in such a hurry. Don't be so infatuated with him and in 'lust' that you absolutely lose your mind. I referenced to not lose your mind, because being in love will cause many women to make poor choices. Being in love will cause you to wear blinders. Speaking from experience, oftentimes, we instinctively see the signs and flaws very early on in the relationship. However, we are head over heels in love with the person that we overlook all the signs. We are completely smitten with the person and we don't want to see any flaws in the relationship. You begin to justify it by telling yourself that the flaws you notice are miniscule compared to all the other wonderful things you absolutely love and adore about him. Take a minute and come back to reality.

Don't be overly excited to say that you have a man that you overlook his many defects. By the way, forget about trying to change him once you secure the deal. It usually doesn't work out as you plan. Oftentimes, women enter into relationships and marriages hoping to change the man. When a woman sets out to change her husband, this can often lead to nagging. For example, we want them to change a certain behavior or to do things differently. So, we constantly give them suggestions and advice. We express to them what we think or how we think it should be done. We may as well be honest and admit that we are guilty of doing this sometimes. I know I am. I aim to not be a nagging wife. Lord, help us! The Bible talks about a nagging wife in Proverbs. There's essentially nothing in the world that men hate more than a nagging wife.

> *"Better to live alone in a tumbledown shack than share a mansion with a nagging spouse."*
> *Proverbs 21:9 (MSG)*

We shouldn't try to change the person we choose or have chosen to marry. However, I believe when two people love each other, they will compromise and communicate honestly about any problems or concerns that they may have in the marriage. Communicating these concerns with love and kindness can initiate change in the marriage. Change can occur because there is a sincere desire to make each other happy. The couple should be inspired to always do the work needed to make the marriage thrive.

Now, for those of us who are already married. If you are currently in a marriage, ask yourself this question: Am I getting what I need and deserve from my husband? Does my husband possess the qualities that are essential for a marriage to be successful? Don't go looking "upside" your husband's head because he might not possess all of the qualities listed. Let's be realistic. However, if your husband lacks the qualities and he truly loves you and wants to keep you, he will make the necessary changes to become a better mate. God made men and women to complement each other physically, emotionally, intellectually, and socially. Husbands who are committed will put forth the effort to make his wife happy, and to make her feel safe and secure in their marriage. Marriage isn't easy. It requires time, effort, and work. Husbands who are committed to their wives and their marriage will also strive to be a better husband every single day. They will put in the work.

I'm reminded of the phrase I often see used on social media: *"Understood The Assignment."*

UNDERSTOOD THE ASSIGNMENT: The slang term is a popular way to praise someone who is going above and beyond to do a good job. According to the Urban

Dictionary, "understood the assignment" is a phrase used when someone is giving 110%. It is a phrase used to acknowledge someone who has done an exceptional job or has exceeded expectations.

It is imperative that husbands understand their assignment. God has placed a tremendous responsibility on their shoulders. Husbands are commissioned by God to be leaders, providers, protectors, and companions. For the husbands who may be falling short, I pray that they are encouraged to step up. For the husbands who don't understand their role in a marriage according to the Bible, their marriage could be in potential danger. But, with God's help and guidance, it doesn't have to be. The husband's role in the marriage can essentially determine the fate of the marriage. He is the driving force in the marriage. My husband is the leader in our home. As his wife, I am happy to follow his lead because I know he allows God to lead him. I am able to come into submission in response to my husband leading and loving me as God commanded him to.

I encourage all ladies who are waiting to be found to think about the characteristics you desire in a husband. I've listed a few, but there are many other qualities that are very important to have in a husband. My beautiful sisters, you can decide today, that you will not settle for anything when it comes to your heart. Let '*I will not accept anything less than what I deserve*' be your mantra. You will no longer accept just anything a man gives you. **You don't have to settle. <u>You will not settle. Wait on him.</u>** You know exactly what you desire in a husband. You know your worth and you deserve to be loved, respected, and valued. You deserve to feel secure in your marriage, and you should always be a priority in your husband's life.

I believe a husband who truly loves God will understand his assignment. I truly believe when your husband loves God, he will understand how to love you correctly. He will love you like Christ loved the Church. Let's talk about it!

CHAPTER 1

HE IS A LEADER
(HE ALLOWS GOD TO LEAD HIM)

God Wants Husbands to be LEADERS. One of the primary roles of a husband in the Bible is to lead. When I think of leadership, I think of someone who leads or guides. A God-fearing husband should lead and guide his family. This is a great responsibility. Don't get it twisted, husbands are not dictators who demand their wives to do as they are told. They do not rule over their wives. Instead, husbands should lead and influence their wives and families in accordance with biblical teaching.

"Wives, submit yourselves unto your own husbands, as unto the Lord. For the husband is the head of the wife, even as Christ is the head of the church: and he is the saviour of the body."
Ephesians 5:22-23 (KJV)

"But I would have you know that the head of every man is Christ; and the head of the woman is the man; and the head of Christ is God."
I Corinthians 11:3 (KJV)

Being the head or leader doesn't demand that the wife should obey her husband's every wish or command.

Being the head doesn't make the wife inferior to her husband. God doesn't view women as second-class citizens. A wife's submission to her husband is in response to her love and devotion to the Lord first. She submits to the Lord out of a humble and grateful heart, not because she is a slave, but a servant. Likewise, biblical submission in marriage is servanthood, not enslavement. A Godly wife is motivated to submit to her husband, not out of fear, self-interest, or self-protection, but out of love. She is motivated to yield to her husband because she is confident in his leadership abilities. He displays humility rather than arrogance. He isn't a dictator or ruler in the home who giving orders and commands all day long. He isn't controlling, domineering, or disrespectful to his wife because this is a sin and is out of order. He is the Godly leader in the home who has been given the authority and the responsibility to lead his family as God gives him wisdom and direction. You might say to yourself, I'm an adult and I have a mind of my own. I can do whatever I want to do. I can make decisions for myself. Yes, you certainly can, but is this in the will of God? The husband is the leader in the home. We must know our place.

God require husbands to lead their wives and their homes. In order to be a great leader, the husband must have a relationship with God. He must allow God to lead him. A wife will likely have some reservations about following her husband's lead if he isn't following God's lead. I would not follow my husband's lead if he wasn't leading me on the right path. In order for him to be a good leader, he must be a good servant. I follow my husband's lead because he is indeed a servant of God. He loves God and lives for Him. He is saved, sanctified, and Holy Ghost filled. He is honest, trustworthy, responsible, and consistent. He understands his assignment as the leader in our home and he takes his role very seriously. As a result, I am happy to submit to my husband.

Earlier, I encouraged all ladies who were waiting to be found to think about the characteristics they desired in a husband. Ladies, also take a minute and re-examine yourself. Do you want him to lead? Will you allow your husband to lead? Wives must learn how to submit to their husbands. This is the unequivocal Word of God. Wives, you're not expected to get on your knees and bow down to him. That's not what the Bible is telling you to do. The Bible clearly instructs wives to be submissive and allow our husbands to lead the home. God never intended for the wife to be the man of the home or to carry such a heavy burden on her shoulders. Many women today are very independent and often feel they don't necessarily need a man to take care of them. I can speak from experience because I felt the same way for a while. Having gone through a divorce and living on my own for over two years, I was accustomed to taking care of myself. Once I married my husband, I didn't have a problem submitting to him. I found it difficult allowing him to take care of me. By not allowing my husband to take care of me, I hurt his feelings and made him feel unwanted and not needed. I never meant to make him feel this way because I definitely wanted him and needed him in my life. I had to quickly learn how to relinquish some of the control I had and allow my husband the opportunity to truly take care of me.

    God wants husbands to be leaders. **REAL MEN LEAD!** Leadership requires husbands to take the initiative. A good leader is one who talk less and allows his actions to speak for him. Godly leaders are concerned about their families and it prompts them to step up and develop goals, plans, and strategies that will benefit the family. He loves his family and he listens to the voice of God before making decisions. He has been charged with a great responsibility. His obedience to God and the love he has for his family motivates him to lead and take initiative in the home. He doesn't sit idle and wait for his wife to figure it out. He leads by example. He understands how to lead and guide his family on the right path. He demonstrates this by the way he treats you, speaks to you, provides for you, protects you and loves you. As a result of his consistency, he gains your trust and you trust him with your heart. He prays and seeks God for divine guidance for his family. Therefore, you are willing to submit yourself to him as his wife and his helpmeet. Ultimately, this brings peace and value to the marriage, and glory and honor to God.

What do you do, if you find that your husband isn't allowing God to lead him? Are you supposed to quietly follow him? This can be a challenging situation. You know what the Bible says about the husband being the head and the leader of the family. You want to be obedient and submissive to your husband, right?

SCENARIO: Husband has missed the car payment for the last two months. The creditor has been calling repeatedly to collect payment or to schedule a payment arrangement. Husband has been ignoring the calls for the last few weeks. The creditor is now calling his place of employment since he refuses to answer his personal phone. Husband is very frustrated because he's getting calls at his job. This causes husband extreme stress and embarrassment. Husband still hasn't made a car payment. The creditor calls his personal phone again. Husband asks his wife to answer the phone and tell the creditor that the car payment has been mailed. Should the wife obey her husband?

In this scenario, the husband isn't demonstrating leadership qualities. He isn't allowing God to lead him. He is putting his character and his integrity in jeopardy. He is asking his wife to lie for him. He is asking his wife to be deceptive, which is not of God. In this situation, the wife should definitely not comply with her husband's request. If she had complied, she would've also jeopardized her integrity. She would've chosen to lie for her husband, which is clearly a sin. Remember, I stated that I will follow my husband as he follows Christ. If, for some reason, he ever decided to not follow Christ or make decisions that are clearly contrary to the Word of God, I will have no part of it. Certainly, it is very important for a wife to support her husband. However, in this particular scenario, the wife could support her husband by reminding him of the Word of God, in hopes that he would repent, reconsider his request, and make the right decision. Satan is a deceiver. He never sleeps and he is always on his job. He attacks you at your weakest state. He knows when you're vulnerable and he waits for the perfect opportunity to attack us or try to tempt us. In times of temptation, we must not allow ourselves to fall into the traps that the devil set for us. We have to rebuke Satan in the name of Jesus. We have to remind ourselves of what God says in His Word. The enemy doesn't mean us any good. He will try to destroy us, but God is our help in time of trouble!

> ❧
> *"The thief cometh not, but for to steal, and to kill, and to destroy: I am come that they might have life, and that they might have it more abundantly."*
> *John 10:10 (KJV)*

CHAPTER 2

❦

HE LOVES HIS WIFE
AS HE LOVES HIMSELF

God Wants Husbands To Be LOVERS. A husband is commanded to love his wife unconditionally. Jesus Christ gave everything He had, including His own life for us. This is the standard of unreserved, selfless, and sacrificial love that husbands are commanded to have for their wives. Marriage is God joining two people together, and the two becoming as one. People often refer to marriage as "tying the knot." The meaning of "tying the knot" is to get married to someone, or the performance of a marriage ceremony. In many cultures around the world, knots are used as a symbol of unity. While this phrase could stem from a symbolic knot, physical knots have actually been used in marriage ceremonies. Marriage isn't merely two people tying the knot. Marriage is God joining two people together, and the two become as one. When a husband and wife get married, they become one flesh. The husband and wife are a part of each other.

Because the husband is one with his wife, he must treat her the way that he would treat his own body. Therefore the husband should love his wife as he loves himself. He should take care of his wife as he would take care of himself. He wouldn't do anything to deliberately hurt or destroy himself. Thus, he should never hurt or destroy his wife in any way. He who loves his wife loves himself.

"So ought men to love their wives as their own bodies. He that loveth his wife loveth himself. For no man ever yet hated his own flesh; but nourisheth and cherisheth it, even as the Lord the church: For we are members of his body, of his flesh, and of his bones."
Ephesians 5:28-30 (KJV)

Paul expressed in these verses that husbands are instructed to love their wives. The husband is to love his wife because she is his body. They are one flesh and they are no longer separate from each other. Biblically speaking, a husband and wife are more related to each other than they are to those who actually share their

DNA. The love God commands the husband to have for his wife here in these passages is not a love that comes or goes with feelings or emotions. This love doesn't have any conditions or restrictions. This love is an act of will and determination. It is a conscious decision to love regardless and unconditionally. The husband's role in marriage is to love his wife just as much as Christ loves the church. I came across a perfect example of how a husband should love his wife. It will help you to understand the gravity of love a husband should have for his wife. I will share a snippet with you.

I heard of a man once who really loved his wife, but he also wanted to please God, and he was scared that he loved his wife too much. He didn't want to make an idol out of her. So he went and talked to his pastor, and this wise pastor took the man to this passage (Ephesians 5:25b) and had the man read it. Then the pastor asked the man, "Do you think that Christ loves the church too much?" "No," said the man. "Do you think that you love your wife as much as Christ loves the church?"

"No," said the man again. "Then," said the pastor, "you need to love your wife more, not less. You have not loved your wife as much as you should until you love her as much as Christ loves us."
~Author Unknown

A husband should be attentive to his wife. He should always do his best to set aside time to spend with his wife, talk to her, laugh with her, and enjoy her company. She is a precious gift from God, that is given to love, comfort, support and encourage her husband. In doing so, the relationship has the opportunity to grow and flourish. It also helps to build an even stronger and successful marriage. The husband is commanded to love his wife unconditionally. Scripture tells him to love her as Christ loved the church.

"Husbands, love your wives, even as Christ also loved the church, and gave himself for it;"
Ephesians 5:25 (KJV)

Husbands should honor their wives. He should be willing to give up everything for his wife. He should love his wife because she deserves it. He should love and cherish her above everyone else. Aside from God, she should be the most important person in her husband's life. He should nourish and cherish her. He should never be harsh or cruel to his wife. He is warm and loving with his wife, showing honor to her as the weaker vessel. This is how God has intended for husbands to interact with their wives.

Christ loved us so much that He made the ultimate sacrifice for us. His love is the perfect example of selfless and sacrificial love. It is the kind of love that is put into action. Christ demonstrated His love for us by dying for us.

"But God commendeth his love toward us, in that, while we were yet sinners, Christ died for us."
Romans 5:8 (KJV)

Communication is very important in a relationship. It is very important for me to be able to communicate in my marriage. There was a time in my life when I didn't communicate very well. I was silent even when I didn't want to be. I didn't speak up for myself for many years. I didn't have a voice. Today, I have a voice and I don't have a problem using it. Open and honest communication is critical in a marriage. I am definitely a great communicator in my marriage. My husband might say I talk too much sometimes! I accept the constructive criticism from my husband. I'm very thankful that he loves me so much that he allows me to always have a voice in our marriage. I'm able to communicate with my husband about anything. It is very important for wives to know that they can talk to their husbands about anything. Husbands should always love their wives so dearly that they feel comfortable sharing anything with them without fear or judgement. Husbands should always be there to listen to their wives. They should not only listen with their ears but, more importantly, with their heart.

A Husband loves his wife as he loves himself when he prioritizes her happiness. His wife's happiness takes precedence over his own happiness. He has an unconditional love for her. He thinks about his wife and children, if any, first before he thinks of himself; my husband sure does. He is happy and he makes sure that I'm happy as well. This is what marriage and being committed to one another is all about. We are two individuals viewing our marriage as an opportunity to love and honor one another. We desire to please God and make each other happy. To God, be the Glory!

I would be remiss if I didn't mention this next topic in my book. Here goes: While our husbands are commanded to love us, we must make sure we are making it easy for them to love us. We have to make sure we're holding up our end of the deal in the marriage. He is the king of the house. Therefore, he should be treated as such. In the midst of daily life, routine, work, and family, our lives change. Our priorities and our schedules often change. We, perhaps, become extremely comfortable and complacent in our marriages. We begin to neglect our husbands in areas where they need us most; not necessarily sexual needs. (Of course, sex is an important need.) The intimate one on one time you spent together has dwindled. You're in one room watching television and he's in another room. Sure, there's nothing wrong with this - but this shouldn't be something that happens every single day. Sit and watch television together from time to time.

    We need our husbands, and they need us, too. Men want to be loved and appreciated just as much as we do.

It's not asking too much for us to encourage and support our husbands. Tell him how proud you are of him. They need to hear words of affirmation from us. It means a lot to our husbands when we become their biggest cheerleader.

Listen…. Women have a natural desire for love and affection. Whereas men have a natural desire to be respected. Always respect your husband. Wives are called to respect and be submissive to their husbands. Allow him to be the man. Make him feel like a man. Allow him to lead. It was in God's original design for husbands to lead. Let him perform his God given assignment. When we allow our husbands to lead, it doesn't diminish our worth or our role as wives. We should love and respect our husbands as leaders in the home. A wife respects her husband by expressing appreciation for how hard he works to care for his family.

A wife can also respect her husband by admiring him, looking up to him, and holding him in high regard.

"The wife must see to it that she respects and delights in her husband that she notices him and prefers him and treats him with loving concern, treasuring him, honoring him, and holding him dear."
Ephesians 5:33b (AMP)

Remember to thank your husband for being a great provider. He probably already knows that you're thankful for the hard work and sacrifices that he makes to provide for you, and the family, but he also needs to hear it from you. Thank him for the many provisions that he makes for the family. Show him how much you truly appreciate him. Yes, Ma'am, I gas my husband all the way up! I want him to always know how I feel about him. He doesn't have to wonder. Try it. He will appreciate it and love you for it.

CHAPTER 3

HE IS A PROVIDER

A man instinctively feels a strong desire to provide for his family. He needs to provide in order to feel like he's a man. His ego takes an enormous hit if he can't provide for those that he loves. A provider involves assuming responsibility for meeting the needs of the family. Paul tells us in 1Timothy 5:8, "But if anyone does not provide for his own, and especially for those of his household, he has denied the faith, and is worse than an unbeliever."

"But if any provide not for his own, and specially for those of his own house, he hath denied the faith, and is worse than an infidel."
I Timothy 5:8 (KJV)

The Bible instructs husbands to provide for their families. He should work and earn enough money to adequately provide all the essential needs of his wife and children. The Bible doesn't say that the wife isn't allowed to assist her husband financially. She can definitely assist in supporting the family. A good wife will help ease the burden of her husband if needed. How selfish it would be for a wife to watch her husband go to work every day and is aware that he is struggling and straining to adequately provide for the family and doesn't attempt to assist him. Doesn't she know they can be so much 'better together?' Doesn't she know that they can accomplish more when they work together?

> ***"The wise woman builds her house, but with her own hands the foolish one tears hers down."***
> ***Proverbs 14:1(NIV)***

Although the Bible emphasizes that husbands are the providers, it is equally important to acknowledge the biblical perspective of marriage being a joint partnership and support system within the family. The husband is tasked with the responsibility of being the provider for the family. As the provider, he should place the needs of his wife and family above his own. Let's also consider the collaboration between spouses, where both husband and wife contribute to the well-being and success of their family. The current year is 2023 and we know that within the last few years everything has 'gone up.' Food prices have increased. Gas prices are soaring. The dollar store is a thing of the past. If the family's income isn't within a certain tax bracket, it will likely require dual incomes to support the family. The husband's role is to be the provider, but he might need his wife's assistance. It's perfectly fine for the wife to ease the burden for her husband. The husband and wife are one. Why should the financial burden be placed solely on the husband when his wife is there and can assist him? A marriage is a partnership and you are building a life together.

> ***"And the Lord God said, It is not good that the man should be alone; I will make him an help meet for him."***
> ***Genesis 2:18 (KJV)***

It is extremely important to be financially responsible in the marriage. For a husband or wife to spend money without regard to the family's financial situation is irresponsible. This will put a tremendous amount of strain on the marriage. Financial responsibility involves sitting down and having a conversation. The husband and wife should discuss the budget, goals for the family, and the plans to reach the goals together. A husband and wife must be on one accord when it comes to the family's finances. Always consult with the other before making large purchases. Large purchases warrant a conversation in our home. My husband and I are one and what affects one, affects the other.

My husband and I are a dual income family. We're in a position where I can afford to pamper myself and purchase some of the nicer things that I want. You've heard the clichés; "*You only live once.*" (YOLO), "*You *only have one life to live. You may as well enjoy it."* My husband often says, *"You'll never see a U-Haul behind a hearse."* In other words, when our time has expired on Earth, we can't take any possessions with us. If I want something in particular, I can definitely purchase it. I work hard and I deserve it. The message I want to convey is that before any extremely large purchases are made, I have a conversation with my husband. My husband is the head of our home. He is the leader in the home. He isn't the boss or "Mr. Big and Bad" who runs everything without considering me. That's not who he is. My husband always ask my opinion or for my input on various things. We are in this marriage together. We discuss the pros and cons together. As the leader in our home, he has the final say. Do I always agree with his decision? Absolutely not. Let's be honest, many women can be very emotional and impulsive at times. Well, let me talk about myself. I can be very emotional and very impulsive at times. When I want something, I want it. I don't always think it through. On the other hand, my husband is the exact opposite. He will not make any impulsive decisions. He will definitely pray and seek God first. Ultimately, I trust my husband's decisions and his leadership because I know that he has the family's best interest at heart.

CHAPTER 4

HE IS A PROTECTOR

The husband must be able to defend what God has given him. The Bible tells us in I Peter 5:8 to ***"Be sober, be vigilant; because your adversary the devil, as a roaring lion, walketh about, seeking whom he may devour."*** The husband must protect his wife from the enemy's attack. He must protect his wife from any harm. Although we think we are very capable of taking care of ourselves for the most part the Bible still charge the husband with the responsibility of caring for and protecting his wife. God made men and women differently. Thus, due to the physical nature and strength God gave men, He has charged them with the provision and protection of their families.

Husbands are expected to protect and safeguard their families from harm whether physical, emotional, or spiritual. Protecting us from harm might mean helping us avoid situations where we could potentially be in danger.

It could also mean them standing up for us if someone is being very hurtful or disrespectful.

It is very important to the Godly husband to protect his wife. What man, that takes his position as the head of his family seriously, doesn't feel the need to protect his wife? There is something innately in the man that causes him to question his manhood if he doesn't defend and protect what is his. It's in his DNA to be a protector. Husbands are compelled to protect and shield their wives from the pain and agony that life may bring. A husband uses his strength to protect his wife from any physical harm. He will put himself in harm's way, rather than risk her harm.

The Godly husband will not only protect his wife physically, but he will protect her emotionally. He will protect his wife's heart. He will pay attention to her and learn what truly makes her happy. He will pay attention to what she likes and dislikes. He will love her in a way that doesn't cause her unnecessary stress or break her heart and leave her damaged.

"In the same way, you husbands must give honor to your wives. Treat your wife with understanding as you live together. She may be weaker than you are, but she is your equal partner in God's gift of new life. Treat her as you should so your prayers will not be hindered."
I Peter 3:7 (NLT)

A wife wants her husband to protect her. He should always be her hero. I prayed for a God-fearing man, a man full of faith. I prayed for a husband who would be my holy knight in shining armor; a husband who would not hesitate to bear the sword of the Spirit on my behalf. A husband respects his wife emotionally when he truly understands who she is. He doesn't try to change her. He understands her experiences and loves her in spite of what she's been through. For example, my husband knew that when he found me over nine years ago, I had emotional baggage. He was very loving, gentle, compassionate, and extremely patient with me. He understood that I had difficulty trusting at that time. He understood that I was working through some unresolved trauma. I was very apprehensive and fearful and wasn't confident that I wanted to open up my heart to love again. Needless to say, my husband loved me through my pain, fears, and insecurities. Before I married my husband, he promised to always protect my heart. I'm so happy that I decided to give this man a chance! (LOL)

As the protector, the husband should provide a safe and loving home for his wife and family that will make her feel safe and secure. He will always make sure that she feels safe by protecting her heart. He will shield and protect his wife from any distractions. He should protect his wife and his marriage from anything or anyone who could potentially cause a problem. He should never allow anything or anyone to come between them and their marriage. Don't be deceived because it could happen. Let's be real for a minute. Our husbands have female friends, and they also work with beautiful women every day. There is absolutely nothing wrong with this; they should definitely have friends. However, the husband must always remember that he is a married man. He has to set boundaries when working and interacting with other women. Any relationship that makes the wife feel uncomfortable should be avoided. It isn't always a case of the wife being jealous. It's about the husband being faithful, respectful, and not allowing himself to get "caught up." It is imperative that we shield and protect our marriages as much as possible. Just because we're saved, we're not exempt from being tried and tested. Satan is busy and he wants to destroy our marriages. He has many tricks up his sleeve to entice married men and women to believe that the grass is much greener on the other side. It's a trick of the enemy that has destroyed many marriages. Having clear boundaries are essential for a healthy marriage. Husbands should set clear boundaries with female friends and coworkers. This is a very important way for husbands to protect their wives and their marriages from outside distractions.

While physical protection and emotional protection are important aspects of a husband's role, the Bible also emphasizes the importance of spiritual protection. In Ephesians 6:4, fathers (husbands) are instructed to raise their children in the nurture and admonition of the Lord.

> *"And now a word to you parents. Don't keep on scolding and nagging your children, making them angry and resentful. Rather, bring them up with the loving discipline the Lord himself approves, with suggestions and godly advice."*

Ephesians 6:4 (TLB)

This includes the husband leading the family spiritually, instilling moral values, and shielding them from harmful influences.

Husbands should be able to protect their families from spiritual attacks. He is determined to use the only weapon he knows that will work in his favor. He uses his weapon of prayer. It's the only way to defeat the enemy. He prays fervently for his family. He pleads the blood of Jesus.

> *"The effectual fervent prayer of a righteous man availeth much."*
> ***James 5:16b (KJV)***

Satan is waiting to attack us at any opportunity he gets. 1 Peter 5:8 warns us to "*be alert and of sober mind because the enemy, the devil, is lurking around like a roaring lion looking for someone to devour.*" Satan is looking to destroy us. He is looking to destroy our lives, our children's lives, our health, our homes, our finances, and our marriages. Husbands, who are the leaders in the home, have the responsibility to pray for their families and protect them from any spiritual attacks and danger that the enemy tries to bring. He prays that God will keep the family covered under His blood. Thank God for a praying husband!

> *"He guards the paths of the just and protects those who are faithful to him."*
> *Proverbs 2:8 (NLT)*

CHAPTER 5
HE IS A SUPPORTER

When you're in a healthy marriage, you want to see your spouse live up to their fullest potential. You want your spouse to be successful. Your husband will encourage you to be the best version of yourself. He is your greatest supporter. He stands by you through all the ups and the downs. He's always there to build you up regardless of what you might be going through. He has your back. He covers you. He supports you in every pursuit you attempt. He believes in you and your ability to succeed. He is your number one cheerleader. He's there to listen to you when you doubt your capabilities. His responsibility is to encourage you and reassure you that with God on your side, the possibilities are endless. He is always there to comfort you and confirm his love for you.

Being supportive in a marriage is very important because it is one of the most significant factors for building a stable relationship. Yor husband should be your biggest fan! The husband should verbalize the strengths he sees in his wife to help build her up. When you take time to sit down and discuss your spouse's hopes, dreams, and goals for the future, it confirms the support that you have for them. A husband should always encourage his wife to follow her dreams. His encouragement shows her that he's rooting for her to succeed. If she loves to paint, he can support her by purchasing the supplies that she will need to complete her projects. If she loves to cook, and her dream is to own her own restaurant, he can support her in her endeavor to become a business owner. He should help her to accomplish her goals. By any means necessary he should provide emotional support, offer reasonable assistance as needed, and celebrate her accomplishments.

When I began writing my first book, my husband was very supportive. He took on extra responsibilities in the home which allowed me time to write. He didn't complain much about the amount of time I spent writing. There were many nights I didn't come to bed because I was busy writing. He understood that I was passionate about telling my story. He was definitely my biggest supporter during the entire process. In fact, he purchased the first official copy of my book. This meant so much to me!

Having supportive husbands allow wives to deal with the many challenges that they may face in life. When the wife knows that she can count on her husband to be there when she is struggling with issues, or when she knows that he is always available for her to truly vent after a horrible day at work, she will be confident that she can face whatever life throws her way. Being supportive in a marriage also builds trust. When spouses are supportive, they eventually learn that they can rely on each other in any situation.

When a husband and wife unite, they bring to the union their own identities, character traits, personalities, dreams, and goals. When you're blessed to have a loving husband who supports your dreams and the support is reciprocated, it allows each individual to thrive and become the best version of themself. However, when one party is not a supportive participant in the marriage, it can cause bitterness and resentment.

Supporting your spouse can look different in every marriage. What I view as support may be totally different for the next person. There are several characteristics that describe a supportive spouse. The important traits of a supportive spouse include:

- Being a good listener

- Showing consideration for your spouse's feelings
- Taking time to laugh with your spouse
- Paying attention to your spouse
- Being helpful
- Having the courage to apologize
- Being honest
- Viewing your spouse as your teammate (You're in the marriage together.)

Being supportive in a marriage is crucial, as it establishes trust and a stable foundation. When you have a supportive spouse, you will be certain that you can always depend on him. He isn't wishy-washy. He has your back. At the end of the day, he is your safe space to land.

CHAPTER 6

HE IS FAITHFUL, LOYAL AND TRUSTWORTHY

Husbands should always be faithful to their wives. Marriage is designed to be a covenant. A sacred relationship of love, trust, and respect. The vow you make to one another on your wedding day is a promise to be faithful to one another. You proclaim your love to each other in the presence of God, friends, family, and loved ones. You announce to all that you are in it to win it! You are committed to remaining married until death. You aren't trying to entertain any negative plans or negative comments regarding your marriage. You promised to love each other and be completely devoted to each other through the good times and the bad times.

God honors marriage between a husband and wife. His desire is for married couples to remain married and completely faithful to one another. When you are married, you are no longer two; you are considered as one flesh. What God has joined together, don't allow anyone to separate it.

"Wherefore they are no more twain, but one flesh. What therefore God hath joined together, let not man put asunder."
Matthew 19:6 (KJV)

Today, we are seeing an increase in the divorce rate. Many married couples are headed to divorce court because of infidelity. The inability to remain faithful to one's spouse is one of the most common problems in marriages. You are married now. You must be loyal and dedicated to your wife and respect the vows you made before God. Once you get married, you are off the market. You can't commit to another relationship. Your responsibility is to resist any temptation that you will encounter because you have a *"whole wife"* at home.

When we are married, it's our responsibility to be faithful. We should never engage in any activities that could potentially lead to flirtation. Men are human and they are very visual. They will look, but they should never touch. Actually, if he does look, that is all he should do. According to the Word of God, looking at a woman, other than your wife, lustfully and desiring to have sexual relations with her is a sin. The very desire to have her is already the sin of adultery in the heart. Husbands must be careful not to use any provocative looks or stares, words or gestures that would put them in a situation that could lead to committing a sexual sin.

> ***"But I say unto you, That whosoever looketh on a woman to lust after her hath committed adultery with her already in his heart."***
> ***Matthew 5:28 (KJV)***

Having boundaries are very important in a marriage. Husbands and wives must have boundaries in place. They must respect and honor the boundaries they set in place in order to have a successful marriage.

Boundaries serve as safeguards in a relationship and demonstrate your commitment to honoring each other's needs and desires.

The husband is able to prove his love to his wife by being faithful and trustworthy. It is definitely important for our husbands to tell us that they love us. However, I believe the most compelling illustration of a husband's love will be displayed through his consistent commitment and devotion to his wife. He displays his love when he is dependable, faithful, loyal, and trustworthy. When these character traits are consistently displayed in a marriage, the wife will feel safe and secure in the marriage and in the love that her husband has for her. Simply put, his actions will always speak louder than his words.

> *"My little children, let us not love in word, neither in tongue, but in deed and in truth."*
> *1 John 3:18 (KJV)*

A loyal and trustworthy husband possesses qualities that contribute to the growth and success of the marriage. Faithfulness, commitment, open communication, and accountability are significant characteristics that a husband should possess. You should never have to question your husband's commitment or his ability to remain faithful to you. If you have any doubts, this can be extremely problematic in a marriage. I've often heard the cliché: *"Those who have nothing to hide, hide nothing."* I totally agree with this cliché. Why hide things and keep secrets in a marriage? Having secrets and being deceptive will destroy a marriage. What's done in the dark will eventually come to light. Your marriage will thrive when there is total transparency.

"For there is nothing covered, that shall not be revealed; neither hid, that shall not be known."

Luke 12:2 (KJV)

Effective and transparent communication is an essential aspect of loyalty and trustworthiness in marriage. A husband who prioritizes open and honest dialogue fosters an environment where trust can thrive.

"One who walks in integrity walks securely, But one who perverts his ways will be found out."
Proverbs 10:9 (NASB)

When the husband keeps his word, fulfills his promises, and follows through with obligations and commitments, he demonstrates that he can be trusted. When his words and actions are consistent, it provides a sense of safety and security within the marriage. I'm a firm believer that when a man is truly saved and loves God, he will love you correctly. When he loves God, he is honest and transparent. He doesn't cheat. He doesn't flirt with other women. He is faithful to you. As a result, you are able to trust him. You won't feel the compulsive need to know where he is at all times. You won't worry about what he's doing, or who he's with when you're apart. You won't have the constant urge to check his phone. You won't need to know, because you trust him and he's never given you a reason not to trust him. When your husband loves and cherishes you, as his wife and the love of his life, he will make a daily decision to love and respect you. He will not disrespect the marriage covenant. Not only does he want to stay in the will of God, he doesn't want to lose his *good thing.* His good thing is his wife.

"Lying lips are an abomination to the Lord: but they that deal truly are his delight."
Proverbs 12:22 (KJV)

CHAPTER 7
HE ONLY HAS EYES FOR YOU

Do you remember the feelings you had when you first started dating someone? Do you remember the butterflies in your stomach because you really liked him? You had a nervous feeling in your stomach because you really enjoyed spending time with that person. The beginning of a new relationship can be very exciting. The relationship is very exhilarating because it's "brand new." It's new and filled with possibilities. During this stage, the new couple is presenting the best version of themselves. They are usually on their best behavior.

According to research, the constant excitement of new love produces a lot of dopamine. Dopamine is known as the feel-good neurotransmitter. It is the primary neurochemical responsible for the experiences of attraction, love, and desire. The brain releases dopamine when you are experiencing these feelings. Dopamine is responsible for body changes associated with attraction.

When you're around someone you have strong romantic feelings for, you may notice your pulse quicken, your breathing gets shallow, or your cheeks warm up. These are all biological processes that are partially caused by increased levels of dopamine. Your dopamine levels instantly increase because you've detected something desirable in your environment. You are instantly focused and excited by the person you see. You have developed an attraction.

    A husband who only has eyes for his wife exhibits exclusive devotion to her. He dedicates his love, attention, affection, and admiration solely to her. When your husband has eyes only for you, he will make you feel as if you're the most beautiful woman in the world. In his eye, you should be the most beautiful woman in the world. You're a part of him. He will also make you feel wanted and desirable. He will give you compliments.

I know we are accustomed to hearing compliments. We probably hear them daily from other people. How many of you know that a compliment "hits differently" when we hear it from the man that truly loves and adores us? I can tell you from experience, it is always nice to hear compliments from my husband. After eight years of marriage, he still gives me butterflies! He is my "most favorite" person in the whole wide world!

When your husband has eyes only for you, he will put your happiness and well-being ahead of his own happiness as well as anyone else's happiness. He will choose you above anyone else, every single day. My husband checks in with me throughout day. He calls me multiple times a day to talk about absolutely nothing. I love to get his calls. It's perfectly fine with me because this is what we do every day. This is our time together. We have strived to have our daily time together and our daily conversations since the day we met. On the days he is extremely busy and doesn't get the opportunity to check in as often, I really miss talking to him. I've become so accustomed to talking to him four or five times a day. My husband sends me random "I love you" texts, or heart emoji's while at work. His random texts always make me smile. This may not seem like a big deal to many, but a simple heart emoji actually says a great deal. It says he loves me and he's thinking of me. I thought, at one point, that all the "mushy stuff" and the "lovey dovey" phase would eventually taper off. You know how it is when you first get married; you can't seem to get enough of your spouse. I'm sure you can remember the tingly feeling you had in your stomach in the beginning of your relationship and marriage. I'm telling you, there is absolutely no reason it should ever go away. Thankfully, the flame hasn't burned all the way out for us! My mother would often say, "*Marriage is what you make of it.*" I found her advice to be very true. Marriage is work and we must put in the work. In order to have a successful marriage, we must be intentional. We must nurture and cultivate our marriages. Oftentimes, it's the little things you do for each other and with each other that keeps you balanced and connected. Many years ago, I heard a missionary give sage advice to the young married ladies in church. She said, if you and your husband are having a disagreement and are angry with each other, you need to fix it before he leaves home. She said to never let your husband leave home angry or unsatisfied. Don't let him leave home angry and you're not in agreement or on one accord. Make sure your husband leaves home happy because there are some bold and thirsty women outside waiting and wanting to make him happy. (The saintly missionary didn't exactly use the term thirsty, but I'm sure you get my drift.) Ladies, make sure your husband is happy and content. I certainly agree with the missionary's wise counsel. It's excellent advice to make sure your husband is happy and content before he leaves for work. He will appreciate it. His entire day will be so much better. Trust me, you will appreciate it, as well. If you leave for work before he does, give him a big hug and kiss before you head out. Now that I'm retired, I'm usually in the bed asleep when my husband gets ready to leave for work. Before he leaves, he makes sure to kiss me and tell me that he loves me every morning. Small, thoughtful gestures can show your spouse that you love them, care about them, and appreciate them. We all need reassurance from time to time.

    I talked earlier about how the beginning of a new relationship can be very exciting. The both of you are enamored with each other. He thinks you are the best catch ever. He only has eyes for you. This is awesome! I think it is important for us to make sure that we keep his attention. I certainly want to keep my husband's attention. You must remember that men are very visual. You can be an all-around great person, educated, great sense of humor, saved, sanctified, and filled with the Holy Ghost - and most men still want to be with someone who they are physically attracted to. I certainly don't blame them because I would as well. I enjoy waking up every morning to my husband who is easy on the eyes. I believe it is important for us wives to make sure we look beautiful for our husbands. Remind him often of what he has at home waiting on him. I'm not saying that you have to always dress like you're the next top model, but please put some effort into the way you look and the way you present yourself daily. Don't let your husband come home in the evening and see you the same way he left you that morning. Ladies, get up, take a shower, get dressed, and comb your hair. Put on something that your husband likes. Wear an outfit that compliments your figure. I don't mean wear clothes that are so skin-tight that you can hardly breathe. Wear an outfit that makes you look and feel attractive. Spray on some perfume and wait for him to come home. Greet him at the door with a kiss and ask him about his day. Even if you don't necessarily want to hear about his day, ask him anyway. They want us to show genuine interest in them. I'm trying to help somebody! Give that man your undivided attention. Ladies, we should make the effort to stay attractive for our husbands. There's nothing wrong with us wanting to look good for our husbands and wanting to please them in every way.

> *"She that is married careth for the things of the world, how she may please her husband."*
> 1 Corinthians 7:34b (KJV)

Remaining steadfast in fidelity and resisting temptations is a hallmark of a husband who only has eyes for his wife. Proverbs 6:25 (NIV) cautions, "*Do not lust in your heart after her beauty or let her captivate you with her eyes.*" This verse highlights the importance of husbands guarding their hearts and minds against temptation. (I know I've focused on this topic quite a bit, but it is important.) A husband who resists temptation demonstrates his commitment to his wife's trust, while preserving the sanctity and intimacy of their marital relationship.

I am not oblivious to the fact that my husband will find other women attractive. He has eyes and he sees them; but he also knows he has an attractive and devoted wife by his side. (Flips hair) Of course, I'm not blind either. I certainly notice handsome men, as well. However, I know I have a handsome and committed husband right by my side. We all can glance, but we know that's as far as it should go.

> *"Ye have heard that it was said by them of old time, Thou shalt not commit adultery: But I say unto you, That whosoever looketh on a woman to lust after her hath committed adultery with her already in his heart."*
> *Matthew 5:27-28 (KJV)*

Don't fall for the tricks of the enemy. It's never worth losing out with God! Sin disconnects us from the power of God. Sin separates us from God.

> *"But your iniquities have separated you from your God; your sins have hidden his face from you, so that he will not hear."*
> *Isaiah 59:2 (NIV)*

Ultimately, a husband with eyes only for his wife creates a solid foundation for a lasting and fulfilling marriage. He assures his wife daily that her position in his life is secure and irreplaceable.

CHAPTER 8

HE UNDERSTANDS THE IMPORTANCE OF INTIMACY IN THE MARRIAGE

Intimacy is a vital component of a healthy and fulfilling marriage. It goes beyond physical closeness. It also encompasses an emotional, spiritual, and intellectual connection between a husband and wife. Oftentimes, when people think of intimacy, they often think of sex. Don't get me wrong, intimacy does include physical intimacy. However, many people tend to automatically equate intimacy with sex. Intimacy is about being open and comfortable with your partner, so that you're not afraid to be open and vulnerable. Intimacy occurs without having to say a word. It's the way my husband looks at me from across the room. It's when he stops and gives me a hug and kiss as we pass each other in our hallway. Intimacy is when we sit on the sofa and watch a movie together. After eight years of marriage, my husband and I still hold hands as we ride down the highway. These are simple examples of beautiful and intimate moments between a husband and wife. Intimacy in a marriage involves being close to your spouse. It's about how you connect with each other. There are many people who are in love but are unable to connect with each other on an intimate level.

The Godly husband gives selflessly of himself. He carves out time for his wife. He gives his undistracted time and attention to her. I think this is one area, in particular, that many men today are failing in. Men are extremely busy and are distracted by other things that are monopolizing an extreme amount of their time. It's all a part of life and it can be difficult sometimes for them. But husbands must remember to prioritize the people and the things that are most important to them. One of my husband's hobbies is watching television. He spends an enormous amount of time watching television. I don't have a problem with him watching television. I have a problem with him when I feel he's watching the television more than he's watching me. Hello, watch me. Seriously, a simple conversation usually solves this dilemma. The television doesn't come before me.

Physical Intimacy: Physical intimacy is an essential aspect of a marital relationship. It involves the expression of love and desire through affection, touch, and sexual intimacy. Physical intimacy is the type most people think about when they hear the word "intimacy." It refers to the sexual activity typical of a healthy relationship that should occur between a **husband and wife.** (Somebody will catch that. This is a Word for someone.) Physical intimacy strengthens the emotional bond between a husband and wife, fostering feelings of closeness, security, and fulfillment. It is a unique way for spouses to communicate love and care for one another, promoting a sense of unity and deepening the marital connection.

Physical intimacy is very important in a marriage. How many times have you heard people say, *"Marriage isn't all about sex."* You've probably heard this statement more times than you actually realize. I agree with this statement wholeheartedly. Sex isn't everything, but it is definitely important in a marriage. Listen....Who wants to be in a sexless marriage? I certainly don't! I want to encourage all married couples to embrace sex, enjoy sex and have as much sex as you'd like. You are married and it is not a sin. Making love to your spouse is a wonderful way to bless your marriage!

> *"May your fountain be blessed, and may you rejoice in the wife of your youth. A loving doe, a graceful deer, may her breasts satisfy you always, may you ever be intoxicated with her love."*
> *Proverbs 5:18-19 (NIV)*

Emotional Intimacy: Having an emotional connection creates a strong emotional bond between husband and wife. It allows them to share their deepest thoughts, feelings, and vulnerabilities with one another. Emotional intimacy builds a sense of trust and understanding, providing a safe space where both partners can be their authentic selves. This allows both individuals to let their guard down and share intimate or highly personal details without the fear of the other person judging them negatively. The level of trust, communication, and emotional investment that occurs between two people is very important in a marriage. This connection helps spouses support and comfort each other during challenging times; and experience joy and celebration together during moments of triumph. To develop emotional intimacy, the husband and wife must continue to learn, understand, and empathize with who their spouse is on the inside. Ways to achieve emotional intimacy include:

- Communicating daily with your spouse.

- Being vulnerable with your spouse.
- Showing concern for your spouse.
- Being emotionally available for your spouse.
- Expressing appreciation for your spouse.

Spiritual Intimacy: Intimacy also extends to the spiritual dimension of a marriage. Developing spiritual intimacy is the foundation for a lasting marriage. Shared beliefs, values, and spiritual practices create a unique bond between a husband and wife. Engaging in prayer, worship, and spiritual discussions together can deepen the spiritual connection and provide a sense of shared purpose and meaning in the marriage. Spiritual intimacy is very important in a marriage. It is such a blessing to have a saved husband who knows how to go to God in prayer. He prays and pleads the blood of Jesus over our lives and our home. When I'm sick or just desire special prayer, my husband anoints my head with oil and prays for me. God is faithful and He comes to see about His children. This is a wonderful demonstration of spiritual intimacy.

> *"Is any sick among you? let him call for the elders of the church; and let them*
> *pray over him, anointing him with oil in the name of the Lord: And the prayer of faith shall save the sick, and the Lord shall raise him up; and if he have committed sins, they shall be forgiven him."*
> *James 5:14-15(KJV)*

Spiritual intimacy refers to the feeling of trust and unity between the husband and wife, and their faith. It's very likely that when most couples can't seem to connect on an intimate level, the actual issue usually lies in their inability to connect emotionally and spiritually.

> *"Be ye not unequally yoked together with unbelievers: for what fellowship hath righteousness with unrighteousness? and what communion hath light with darkness?"*
> *2 Corinthians 6:14(KJV)*

Spiritual intimacy serves as a foundation for an intimate connection between a husband and wife. Spiritual intimacy in marriage is the divine union between a husband and wife as they become one in mind, body, and spirit. A 2016 study found that connecting a marital relationship to a relationship with a higher power can contribute to the overall well-being of a couple.

Spiritual intimacy occurs when a husband and wife surrender their lives and their marriage to God. You will grow together spiritually when you live for God and He is the third chord in your marriage. Your relationship is based upon living according to God's will and aiming to please Him in all things.

*"And one standing alone can be attacked and defeated,
but two can stand back-to-back and conquer;
three is even better,
for a triple-braided cord is not easily broken."
Ecclesiastes 4:12 (KJV)*

Prayerfully, you are able to understand the power spiritual intimacy can have on your relationship with your spouse. Emotional and physical attraction is what draws you together, but the spiritual connection is what keeps you together.

Benefits of spiritual intimacy in a marriage include:

- It allows you to celebrate love.
- It allows you to connect at the deepest level.
- It connects you with God's purposes and plans for you.
- It allows you to bless each other with God's love.
- It brings your deepest values and desires into agreement.
- It opens the door to the deepest levels of communication.
- It enables your marriage to survive.

CHAPTER 9

HE UNDERSTANDS THE IMPORTANCE OF SEX IN A MARRIAGE

We've discussed earlier that the Godly husband is required to be a leader, provider, protector, and supporter. All of the requirements discussed are important. However, he also needs to be a lover for his wife. This goes both ways. The wife is expected to reciprocate.

Caveat: Don't be so deep that we can't talk about sex...

Sex is *holy* and *sacred* between a husband and wife. Sex is a vital aspect of a fulfilling and healthy marriage. It serves as a unique and intimate expression of love, desire, and connection between a husband and wife.

Marriage is honourable in all, and the bed undefiled.
Hebrews 13:4a (KJV)

Sexual intimacy is a beautiful culmination of the oneness married couples can experience. When we make conscious efforts to connect and become one as a couple, this union is the epitome of becoming *"one flesh."*

For this cause shall a man leave his father and mother, and shall be joined unto his wife, and they two shall be one flesh.
Ephesians 5:31 (KJV)

Sex is a significant aspect of marital relationships today. A husband who understands the importance of sex in a marriage plays a vital role in fostering a fulfilling relationship. Sexual intimacy enhances the emotional connection, meets each partner's needs, promotes well-being, and provides an avenue for communication and exploration.

Physical and Emotional Connection: The husband and wife's relationship shouldn't be predicated on sex. However, it is important in the marriage. Sexual intimacy creates a unique physical and emotional bond between husband and wife. It allows them to express their love, desire, and vulnerability in a deeply intimate manner. A husband who understands the importance of sex recognizes that it fosters a sense of connection and closeness, promoting emotional intimacy within the marriage. It provides a unique opportunity for husbands to express their love, tenderness, and desire for their wives. Engaging in sexual activity strengthens the marital bond and affirms the love and commitment shared between the husband and wife.

Fulfillment of Sexual Needs: A husband who acknowledges the importance of sex in a marriage understands the significance of fulfilling each other's sexual needs. Men and women are totally different. God created men and women with natural, physical, and emotional differences. Usually, where one is weak, the other is strong. The sexual drives of the husband and wife might differ significantly. Therefore, a husband and wife can help each other by meeting the other person's needs through physical and emotional intimacy. 1 Corinthians

7:3-5 confirms the importance of mutual sexual fulfillment, asserting: "*The husband should fulfill his marital duty to his wife, and likewise the wife to her husband. Do not deprive each other except perhaps by mutual consent and for a time, so that you may devote yourselves to prayer. Then come together again.*"

**"*Nevertheless, to avoid fornication, let every man have his own wife, and let every woman have her own husband. Let the husband render unto the wife due benevolence: and likewise also the wife unto the husband. The wife hath not power of her own body, but the husband: and likewise also the husband hath not power of his own body, but the wife. Defraud ye not one the other, except it be with consent for a time, that ye may give yourselves to fasting and prayer; and come together again, that Satan tempt you not for your incontinency.*"
*1 Corinthians 7:2-5 (KJV)***

Husbands should prioritize having an intimate sexual relationship with their wives. It's very important for them to connect with their wives on a physical level. Not only does intimate time spent together satisfy each other's physical needs, but it also strengthens the marriage. By actively prioritizing and meeting each other's sexual needs, it draws you closer together; so, make sure you make time for each other. Sometimes, that might mean spontaneously taking a few minutes together before work. It could mean scheduling date nights. It doesn't matter as long as you get an opportunity to spend quality time together.

Expressing Love and Desire: God's purpose for sex goes far beyond procreation or producing offspring. God created sex so married couples could fulfill His direct command found in Genesis 1:28a. *"And God blessed them, and God said unto them, Be fruitful, and multiply, and replenish the earth."* God's purpose for sex also serves as a means of marital pleasure for married couples. The Song of Solomon has a plethora of passages that describe how a husband and wife can explore and enjoy each other physically. A few verses that confirm this are:

- *"Kiss me again and again, for your love is sweeter than wine." Song of Solomon 1:2 (TLB)*

- *"My beloved one is a sachet of myrrh lying between my breasts." Song of Solomon 1:13 (TLB)*

- *"Like an apple tree among the trees of the woods, so is my beloved among the sons. I sat down in his shade with great delight, and his fruit was sweet to my taste." Song of Solomon 2:3 (KJV)*

- *" Your breasts are like twin fawns of a gazelle, feeding among the lilies." Song of Solomon 4:5 (TLB)*

Sex is a unique expression of love, desire, and attraction between husband and wife. It provides a physical language to express affection, passion, and deep connection. Engaging in sexual intimacy allows couples to communicate their love and desire for one another in a profound and intimate way that cannot be replicated through other forms of expression. It reinforces the love, attraction, emotional and romantic connection within the marriage. Sex also helps with intimacy because it shows that you are still sexually attracted to your spouse. Showing your spouse that you love them and that you desire them is exciting and refreshing for the marriage!

Stress Relief and Emotional Well-Being: Sex is not only pleasurable but also has been shown to have numerous physical and emotional benefits. Sex contributes to your physical and mental well-being. Engaging in regular sexual activity releases endorphins and reduces stress, leading to improved mood and overall mental health. A husband who understands the importance of sex in a marriage recognizes that regular sexual intimacy contributes to the overall health and happiness of both partners. Studies suggests that sex can be a good cardiovascular exercise. It's been known to lower blood pressure, burn calories, and increase heart health, just to name a few. Sex provides a means of pleasure, enjoyment, and relaxation. Notice how you feel after making love to your spouse. Oftentimes, you are more relaxed and ready to go straight to sleep!

Communication and Exploration: Understanding the importance of sex in a marriage involves effective communication and a willingness to explore and understand each other's desires and preferences. A husband who values sexual intimacy actively engages in open and honest discussions about each other's needs, desires, and boundaries. A healthy and active sex life is wonderful for a marriage. Generally, having regular sex and continuing to please one another will lead to a better overall relationship. I think we all will agree that when both the husband and wife are sexually and emotionally satisfied, there is less tension and conflict in the home.

"Let the husband render to his wife the affection due her, and likewise also the wife to her husband."
1 Corinthians 7:3 (NKJV)

CHAPTER 10

HE IS GRATEFUL AND APPRECIATES HIS WIFE

The husband who really wants to make his wife happy will ensure that her emotional love tank is full. He recognizes the importance of showing her unconditional love. He understands that love is not merely a feeling, but an action. He actively expresses his love for her through both words and deeds. He showers her with love and affection. By speaking words of affirmation, expressing gratitude, and displaying affection, a husband creates an environment where his wife feels cherished, valued, appreciated, and deeply loved.

The husband who really wants to make his wife happy will ensure that her emotional love tank is overflowing. One of the best ways to do that is to affirm and acknowledge her frequently. Let her know verbally that you love and value her. Let her know that you truly respect her. It's normal for us to want reassurance from our husbands. We want to always feel loved and appreciated by our husbands. We want to feel appreciated for who we are and for all that we do.

The husband can demonstrate his love and appreciation by actively expressing his love to his wife in many other ways. For instance, showing acts of kindness, dedicating quality time, actively listening and displaying empathy, recognizing her accomplishments, and offering simple acts of service. His demonstration of love and appreciation will strengthen the marriage.

Acts of Kindness: Small acts of kindness goes a long way in showing love and appreciation within a marriage. A husband who understands this principle recognizes the significance of thoughtful gestures that demonstrate care and consideration for his wife's happiness. Acts of kindness doesn't always have to be fancy or expensive. Simple acts, such as making us breakfast in bed, surprising us with flowers, or taking care of household chores, can communicate love and appreciation in a tangible way. It will definitely put a smile to our face.

Kindness is one of the fruits of the spirit as discussed in Galatians 5:22. *"But the fruit of the Spirit is love, joy, peace, patience, kindness, goodness, faithfulness."* When you do something nice for your spouse, you feel better and it is likely to be reciprocated. Generally, it's just nice to be nice! Being kind to others is not only good for them and a good thing to do, but it also makes you happy. You've heard the saying, *"What goes around comes around."* Be kind and it will come back to you. Research shows that being kind to others increases our own levels of happiness as well as theirs.

Quality Time: Spending quality time together is an essential aspect of a loving and fulfilling marriage. A husband who values his wife understands the importance of dedicating time to connect and strengthen their marriage. By actively engaging in activities, engaging in meaningful conversations, and creating space for uninterrupted moments of connection, a husband shows his wife that she is a priority in his life. My husband and I enjoy cuddling and watching television together. We enjoy playing a good game of UNO on a Sunday evening after church. It really doesn't matter what you do, as long as you spend time together. Spending quality time together fosters emotional intimacy. When you don't spend adequate time together, it will create distance and cause feeling of detachment, that could potentially cause other problems in the marriage.

Active Listening and Displaying Empathy: A husband who values his wife's feelings, thoughts, and experiences, actively listens and demonstrates empathy. He creates a safe and non-judgmental space for his wife to share her joys, concerns, and challenges. By showing genuine interest, providing emotional support, and validating her experiences, a husband communicates that his wife's emotions and opinions matter to him. Active listening and empathy strengthens the emotional connection between the husband and wife. It is very important for us to feel loved. It is also important for us to know that we are heard, and understood. When having a conversation with my husband and he gets quiet, I tend to reiterate my statement, or my point of view just to make sure he heard and understood me; that's just what I do. He knows me very well.

Recognizing and Celebrating Accomplishments: A husband who understands the importance of showing love and appreciation recognizes his wife's accomplishments, strengths, and efforts. He celebrates her successes, both big and small. He acknowledges her contributions to the family and the marriage. By giving recognition and expressing pride in her achievements, a husband affirms his wife's value and worth. This recognition also helps to build her self-esteem.

Acts of Service: A husband who understands the importance of showing love and appreciation actively engages in acts of service for his wife. He takes the initiative to lighten her load, assist with household tasks, or support her in pursuing her passions and interests. By willingly taking on responsibilities and assisting his wife, without being asked, a husband demonstrates his love and appreciation.

Appreciating your spouse is one of the most important and positive things that you can do for your marriage. Appreciating your spouse can help alleviate feelings of resentment. Husbands should make a habit of expressing his gratitude to you. *"Thank you,"* means a lot to us. He shouldn't assume that you already know that he appreciates you for what you do. Don't let him off the hook. It's okay to communicate your needs to your husband. If he isn't the type that says, *"Thank you,"* express to him that you would really appreciate a *"Thank you,"* sometimes. His display of gratitude will make you feel more appreciated. As a result, you are more inclined to love and serve him because you know that he loves and appreciates you.

> ***"The church serves under Christ, so it is the same with you wives. You should be willing to serve your husbands in everything."***
> ***Ephesians 5:24 (ERV)***

Husbands should let their wives know how much they love and value them. There's no need for the fancy words or eloquent speeches. A simple, *"I love you"* and

"I appreciate you," along with actions to back it up will suffice.

CHAPTER 11

HE KEEPS NO RECORD OF ANY WRONGS (HE IS FORGIVING)

Forgiveness is defined as a conscious, deliberate decision to release feelings of resentment or vengeance toward a person or group who has harmed you, regardless of whether they actually deserve your forgiveness. The Bible speaks extensively about forgiveness and the importance of forgiving others. The Bible encourages us to forgive others, just as God forgives us all. Matthew 6:14-15 states, *"For if you forgive other people when they sin against you, your heavenly Father will also forgive you. But if you do not forgive others their sins, your Father will not forgive your sins."*

> **"For if ye forgive men their trespasses, your heavenly Father will also forgive you: But if ye forgive not men their trespasses, neither will your Father forgive your trespasses."**
> **Matthew 6:14-15 (KJV)**

Forgiveness and the ability to let go of past wrongs are essential components of a healthy and thriving marriage. Forgiveness creates space for emotional healing, encourages personal development, and strengthens the bond between husband and wife. A Godly husband does not keep a record or keep score of any wrongdoings in the marriage. He will always show his wife that he loves her and forgives her. He doesn't hold on to past mistakes. He doesn't hold grudges.

> *"And above all things have fervent charity among yourselves: for charity shall cover the multitude of sins."*
> *1 Peter 4:8 (KJV)*

The Power of Forgiveness: Forgiveness is a powerful tool that promotes healing and restoration within a marriage. A husband who chooses to forgive understands that holding on to past wrongs or mistakes creates emotional barriers and impedes the growth and development of the relationship. He recognizes the importance of letting go of anger, resentment, bitterness, and the need for revenge. He chooses, instead, to extend grace and understanding to his wife. This is what God does for His children. God continues to bless us all and He gives us grace every day. Grace is the unmerited favor of God. We don't earn it, He gives it to us freely. What a mighty God we serve!

Embrace Imperfections: We all must remember that we are not perfect. The Word of God reminds us in Romans: 3:23 that all have sinned, and come short of the glory of God. We all have imperfections. You will not find a perfect marriage anywhere; both husband and wife are not without flaws. There isn't a need to keep score. Mistakes and shortcomings are part of the human experience. Rather than dwelling on past errors or shortcomings, husbands and wives should embrace the failures as opportunities for growth.

Forgiveness and letting go of past wrongs contribute significantly to the development of trust and emotional security within a marriage. By showing his wife that he doesn't hold grudges or keep records of past mistakes, a husband establishes an atmosphere of safety and acceptance. This allows his wife to feel secure in her vulnerability, knowing that her husband will not use past mistakes against her. This also applies to the wife. She should be willing to forgive her husband. When he apologizes for any mistakes, the wife should forgive him with the same spirit. It takes courage to admit when you're wrong. An apology is a result of humility. Therefore, if your husband loves you, he will definitely apologize and in return you do the same.

Moving Forward: A husband who practices forgiveness and doesn't keep records of any wrongs, recognizes the importance of moving forward. He moves forward with the commitment to have a better life together. He doesn't hold any hostility or bitterness in his heart. Holding grudges can affect a relationship tremendously. A grudge is unresolved hurt and anger that needs to be addressed. Usually, when someone is holding a grudge, there is unfinished business, or problems in the relationship that need to be discussed. The husband understands that dwelling on past mistakes only hinders progress and prevents the relationship from flourishing. Extending forgiveness and embracing an *"onward and upward"* mindset is the only way the marriage can succeed.

> *"Let all bitterness, and wrath, and anger, and clamour, and evil speaking, be put away from you, with all malice: And be ye kind one to another, tenderhearted, forgiving one another, even as God for Christ's sake hath forgiven you."*
> *Ephesians 4:31-32 (KJV)*

POV: If you both have made mistakes in the past. Don't bring up those issues again just to defend yourself or prove your point. Learn to move on from the past, especially if the two of you have already resolved the problems and have already forgiven each other. Bringing up past issues only creates new issues.

"No, Christian brothers, I do not have that life yet. But I do one thing. I forget everything that is behind me and look forward to that which is ahead of me. My eyes are on the crown. I want to win the race and get the crown of God's call from heaven through Christ Jesus."
Philippians 3:13-14 (NLT)

CHAPTER 12
❦❦
HE GIVES TIME-OUTS
(HE IS PATIENT)

When searching for a definition of the word **patience**, I found a few I particularly liked.

- **Patience** is the capacity to accept or tolerate delay, trouble, or suffering, without getting angry or upset.
- **Patience** means enduring hardship or misfortune without complaining.
- **Patience** is not only the ability to wait; it's the ability to keep a good attitude while you wait.

We all are guilty of not being patient at times. Frankly, some people will make you lose your patience. However, what matters is how we respond when we are impatient. The Scripture gives us an excellent illustration of what patience entails.

> *"Wherefore, my beloved brethren, let every man be swift to hear, slow to speak, slow to wrath: For the wrath of man worketh not the righteousness of God."*
> *James 1:19-20 (KJV)*

Thank God for a husband who gives time-outs and is patient with his wife. I am definitely thankful for my husband. I can describe myself by using the youngster's vernacular: "*I do too much*" (sometimes). I can be honest and talk about myself. I can be very meticulous about certain things. I want things 'just so'. I will move my husband's things. I will throw some of his things away. I want things done my way sometimes. I'm spoiled and I know it. Through it all, Elder Brown loves me and is super patient with this girl!!!

Patience is a virtue that plays a crucial role in maintaining a healthy marriage. A husband who embodies patience understands the value of restraint, self-control, and empathy when faced with challenges and conflicts within the relationship. He recognizes that patience allows space for understanding, emotional regulation, and the opportunity to address issues with compassion, rather than anger.

Your marriage will have some difficult moments. Giving each other time-outs is a phrase I use because everybody will need a time-out at some point in the marriage. Marriage isn't always peaches and cream. There will be some tests and trials. It is how you choose to respond to those trials that will make or break your marriage. Will you be patient? Will you remain prayerful, calm, and optimistic while going through? Will you be intentional when it concerns your marriage? Patience means holding your peace rather than constantly complaining about the situation. It can be difficult sometimes, but we must listen to the Holy Spirit when He tells us to be quiet.

Taking time-outs in a marriage involves realizing the need for a temporary break in heated moments of conflict or tension. A husband who implements this technique understands that stepping away from a situation can provide both partners with the necessary time and space to cool down, reflect, and gain a clear perspective. My husband often shares with me the sage wisdom that his grandmother shared with him. He tells me: *"Everything that comes up, can't come out."* Everything that comes to our mind, doesn't need to come out of our mouths. A patient and wise person stops to consider what he or she wants to say and how to say it. The Bible tells us we should be slow to speak. When we speak impulsively, without thinking, and in our feelings, we can cause severe damage to occur.

> *"Those who control their tongue will have a long life; opening your mouth can ruin everything."*
> *Proverbs 13:3 (NLT)*

> *"Wherefore, my beloved brethren, let every man be swift to hear, slow to speak, slow to wrath."*
> *James 1:19 (KJV)*

A patient husband understands the importance of managing his own emotions, maintaining a calm demeanor, and avoiding impulsive reactions. I just described my husband in one sentence. I often tell my husband that he has the patience of Job; not in the literal sense, obviously. He is patient, he is kind, he listens attentively and responds appropriately with love. My husband doesn't raise his voice in anger at me. He understands that to do so would be very triggering for me. He always seeks to understand my perspective, while exuding love, patience and endurance. His priority is to make sure I always feel emotionally safe. When I make a mistake, or simply tick him off (which is very rare), it's cool. He never blows up at me. I never fear even the possibility of him going off on me, because I know that's just not who he is. When he speaks to me, he does it gently, calmly, and always considering my feelings.

> *"Love is patient, love is kind.*
> *It does not envy, it does not boast, it is not proud.*
> *It does not dishonor others, it is not self-seeking, it is not easily angered, it keeps no record of wrongs. Love does not delight in evil but rejoices with the truth. It always protects, always trusts, always hopes, always perseveres."*
> *1 Corinthians 13:4-7 (NIV)*

Let me help somebody: The key to dealing with conflict in a marriage is learning when to back off and give each other some space. Know when to stop pushing and let it go. During an intense disagreement, the most sensible thing to do is to walk away from the situation for a few minutes. Once you've gained your composure, then, come back and continue the conversation. Hopefully, you are able to think more rationally.

CHAPTER 13

HE KNOWS HIS WIFE

Have you ever played the Newlywed Game? The Newlywed Game is such a fun game to play with other couples. The goal of this game is to determine how well you really know your spouse. My question is, *"How well does your husband know you?"* It is very important to know who your spouse is. It is very important for your husband to know you. Your husband should know you better than anyone else does. He should know your likes and your dislikes, what makes you happy and what makes you sad. He should know what your hopes, goals, and dreams are. Speaking on a more personal and intimate topic, he should also know what you like, dislike, or prefer in terms of romance and affection. He should know what you like and dislike in the bedroom. What turns you on and off sexually? It's his responsibility to know. Once he's clear about your needs and desires, he should strive to accommodate you. He is now ready to make sure you are thoroughly satisfied in the bedroom, and outside of the bedroom as well.

If your husband wants to improve his relationship with you, it is essential that he knows your love language. The Word found in Luke 6:31(TLB) instructs us to *"treat others as you want them to treat you."* This verse is considered to be the 'golden rule' to live by. We definitely should adhere to this scripture. This scripture is indeed a Word to live and pattern our lives by. It is also just as relevant in our marriages. However, when it relates to how we love and show love to our spouses, we can't use this same principle. Let me explain. We can't assume that our spouses experience love or will feel loved the same way that we do. We both are different individuals with different personalities, thus, we will give and receive love differently. Instead of treating others how we want to be treated, the five love languages encourage us to treat them how they want to be treated. Believe it or not, people give love and receive love very differently.

The five love languages are five different ways of expressing and receiving love. The five love languages include:

1. Words of Affirmation
2. Physical Touch
3. Receiving Gifts
4. Quality Time
5. Acts of Service

Everyone doesn't communicate love in the same way, and likewise, people have different ways they prefer to receive love from others. Some people have more than one love language, and it will likely change over the course of the marriage. If your husband wants to improve his relationship with you, he should learn to speak your love language.

Words of Affirmation: This love language focuses on the *importance of words*. It involves expressing love and affection through verbal compliments, appreciation, and encouragement. People with this language feel loved and cherished when they receive verbal affirmations, compliments, and words of encouragement. Simple, yet sincere expressions like, *"I love you," "You are amazing,"* and *"I appreciate you,"* hold immense significance for them. Frequent digital communication such as daily texting and posting on social media is also important. These expressions of love makes them feel love, understood, and appreciated. People whose love language is words of affirmation, the impact of positive words can boost their self-esteem and strengthen the emotional connection.

Physical Touch: *Physical touch* is a fundamental love language that transcends cultural boundaries. For individuals who resonate with this language, physical affection plays a crucial role in feeling loved and connected. People with this love language feel most loved through physical contact. Physical signs of affection like hugs, kisses, holding hands, cuddling, sex or any soothing touch can convey immense love and security. Physical intimacy and other forms of affection fosters emotional closeness and a sense of being loved, valued, and cherished.

Receiving Gifts: The love language of *receiving gifts* encompasses more than just material possessions. For these individuals, gifts represent symbols of thoughtfulness and consideration. Whether it's a small token of appreciation, or a meaningful present, the act of giving a gift demonstrates that the giver understands and values their preferences and desires. Such gestures can strengthen emotional connections and create lasting memories.

Quality Time: This love language centers on *giving undivided attention* and spending meaningful time together to strengthen the relationship. In the hustle and bustle of everyday life, quality time often becomes a scarce commodity. However, for individuals who cherish this love language, nothing is more precious than undivided attention. Engaging in meaningful conversations, participating in shared activities, and simply being present without the distraction of television, phones, computers, or any other outside interference are ways to nurture the emotional connection between a husband and wife. Quality time allows couples to build intimacy and trust. They will also have the opportunity to get to know each other better.

Acts of Service: Actions speak louder than words for those whose love language is *acts of service*. Unlike those who prefer to hear how much they're cared for, people whose love language is acts of service like to be shown how much they're appreciated. For these individuals, love is best demonstrated through thoughtful gestures, acts of kindness and helpful deeds. Assisting with household chores, running errands, or offering a helping hand during challenging times are wonderful ways to convey affection. When couples invest their time and energy in making life easier for one another, it communicates a profound sense of love and consideration.

5 LOVE LANGUAGES

	HOW TO COMMUNICATE	ACTIONS TO TAKE
Words of Affirmation	Encourage, affirm, appreciate, empathize. Listen actively.	Send an unexpected note, text, or card. Genuinely encourage, and often.
Physical Touch	Non verbal - use body language and touch to express love.	Hug, kiss, hold hands, show physical affection often. Make intimacy a thoughtful priority.
Receiving Gifts	Thoughtfulness, make your spouse a priority, speak purposefully.	Give thoughtful gifts and gestures. Small things matter in a big way. Express gratitude when receiving a gift.
Quality Time	Uninterrupted and focused conversations. One-on-one time is critical.	Create special moments together, take walks and do small things with your partner. Weekend getaways are huge.
Acts of Service	Use action phrases like "I'll help...". They want to know you're with them, partnered with them.	Do chores together or make them breakfast in bed. Go out of your way to help alleviate their daily workload.

1 Peter 3:7 urges husbands to live with their wives in an understanding way. He should be considerate of her feelings. In order to do this, the husband has to understand his wife. He has to know his wife. A husband's responsibility is to stay abreast of these things and know what is happening in his wife's mind, heart, and her life in general. Does he have any idea as to what your goals and desires are? What really makes you happy or frustrated? What are some of your strengths and

weaknesses? What's your favorite color, food, or television show? It is important to take the time to pray, listen, and communicate. I'm reminded of a saying: *"We love best when we listen often."* Husbands must listen to their wives. Listening allows them to know their wives better and love them in a way that makes them feel cherished and respected. Essentially, a husband should understand what makes his wife feel loved and seek to love her that way. He should know how she wants to be treated and strive to treat her that way. Make sure that your husband speaks your love language.

CHAPTER 14

WHAT IS IMPORTANT TO YOU, IS IMPORTANT TO HIM

I've always heard people say that *"talk is cheap!"* I agree with this cliché. Talk is very cheap. Your husband tells you every day that he loves you. He assures you daily that he supports you 100%. He has your back and is *"10 toes down"* when it comes to you. He doesn't play about you. How can you be sure of his love, commitment, devotion, and loyalty to you? The best way to determine that your husband loves and supports you is by observing his behavior.

> **"Little children, let us stop just saying we love people; let us really love them, and show it by our actions."**
> **1 John 3:18 (TLB)**

If it's important to you, it's important to him. What this means in a marriage is that if you are serious and passionate about something, then your husband will do his best to support you. He will support you with his words and with his actions. How many of you know that words alone are cheap and are of no use to us. Sure, words are nice to hear occasionally. However, words are intangible. Actions are real, tangible, and substantial. Actions require time, investment, and energy. If your husband invests in you, prioritizes you, values you and actively demonstrates his love, affection, and desire for you, this says a lot about him. Sadly, there are many wives that are in distress because they aren't getting what they need from their husbands. He may tell you that he loves you and that you are his first priority. But, when you think about it, his words and actions don't align. We all must remember that our words will start to lose value when our actions don't match.

When you're in a marriage, your husband should find a way to make you a priority in his life. If it's important to you, it should be important to him. If spending time together is important to you, he should try to spend time with you. Spending time together is very important. Even if he's super busy, he should still find ways to let you know that he cares and is thinking of you. It could be as simple as taking 5-10 minutes to check in on you during the day. It could be a simple trip to the grocery store together. It could be a spontaneous weekend getaway. It doesn't always have to be anything extravagant. Sometimes, it's not quantity, but quality time spent together that is most important.

If it's important to you, it's important to him. It's very nice and reassuring to know we're loved by our husbands. We know that we are loved and that he is often thinking of us. He's thinking about what we need and what he can do to make us happy. This could be a big or small gesture. It's really the thought that counts. My husband knows I like Starburst Jelly Beans, Mentos, Peanut M&M's and the Lotus Biscoff (airplane) Cookies. These are some of my favorite "zoo-zoo's." (Zoo-Zoo's:

According to my mother, the late Mother Hattie Anderson-Green, this is another word for snacks. It was used when she was a child.) Anyways, my snacks are "important" to me and he wants to make me happy! (The zoo-zoo's will do a number on your figure. Mind your business.)

Whatever is really important to you, should be important to your husband as well. For instance, special days and events are very important to us. Typically, we don't forget special days like our first date, the day our husband proposed, birthdays, wedding anniversaries and other days that are special to us. If we can remember these special days, our husbands can make a better effort to remember them, as well. If he can't remember them all, he should be sure to remember your birthday and wedding anniversary, at least. These are very important dates to remember. Every day is an opportunity for husbands to show how much they love us. However, remembering our special days and special occasions shows us that they're important to them, too.

When we have a problem, our husband has a problem. Our husbands always want to take our pain away. If they could, they certainly would do just that. They hate to see us worry or in pain. They love us and don't want to see us hurting. Even though my husband can't always swoop in and save me from everything that causes me pain and stress - the fact that he wants to, and he really tries his best to make things better for me, melts my heart. Husbands are unable to solve all of our problems. However, when they make themselves available to us, listen attentively to us, allow us to occasionally vent, allow us to cry it out in their arms, support us and reassure us that they have our backs, it means the world to us.

husbands to show how much they love us. However, sometimes it is appreciated on those occasions too when they show us that their attention is not for us.

When we have a problem, our husband's first reaction is to take our pain away. If they could, just remove it and do just that. They hate to see us worry or in pain. On the other hand, I don't want to see us hurting either. So, if my husband can't always "shop in" and save me, and fix up everything that causes the pain and stress — the fact that he wants to, and really tries his best to make things better for me, that may mean. Husbands are unable to solve all of our problems. However, when they listen to themselves, and are willing to just listen attentively to us, allow us to occasionally vent, allow us to cry when in their arms, support us and reassure us that they have our backs, it means the world to us.

- 159 -

CHAPTER 15

HE CONTINUES TO PURSUE YOU

Pursue (Pursuit):
- Pursue: To follow in order to overtake; to engage, chase.
- Pursue: To do something or try to achieve something over a period of time.
- Pursue: To seek to form a relationship with (someone) in a persistent way.
- Pursuit: Interests and attempts to achieve something. To woo or court.
- Pursuit: An effort to secure or attain.
- Pursuit: The act of striving to gain or accomplish something.

What is or was your love story? Take a few minutes to reminisce. How did it start for you?

Scenario: Young man meets young lady. There is an attraction and they share similar interests. They begin to date and spend time together. They develop a connection with one another. Their love continues to grow each day. They're in love and want to spend the rest of their lives together. The young man asks for the young lady's hand in marriage and she eagerly accepts. They get married and begin to share and build a life together.

Honestly, the majority of love stories generally follow the same narrative. During the dating phase, we are pursued fiercely. We are showered with love, attention, flowers, and gifts. You name it, they were right there at our beck and call. Our wish was their command. I know what I'm talking about because this was my experience, as well. (IYKYK… If You Know You Know.) Usually, early in the relationship or during the dating phase, he pursues you with everything in him. He's pulling out all of the cards. Literally; he leaves nothing to chance. The two of you are spending considerable amounts of time together trying to get to each other. He is certain to *"wine and dine"* you. He does everything, within his power, to make you happy. He has one goal in mind; that goal is to make you his wife.

Unfortunately, once you are married and time progresses, the pursuing usually is put on pause, or comes to an end. Of course, this isn't the case for all marriages. There are many marriages where the husband doesn't miss a beat. He is in constant pursuit of his wife. Do you have any idea as to why many husbands slack off or completely stop pursuing and wooing their wives? I gave you several definitions of the words pursue and pursuit. You should know what they mean now. The definitions of the word pursue and pursuit provides possible insight into the reasons why it usually stops after marriage. Look closely at the words used in the definitions above: to achieve, to secure, to attain, to gain, and to accomplish. The pursuit declines, or ends, because the goal has been accomplished. He has successfully achieved, secured, attained, gained that which he set out to accomplish. In other words, he has you now; there isn't any reason to keep pursuing you. His mission is accomplished. He has married you and the deal is sealed. I'm not sure where some men get this foolishness from.

Maybe, it all goes back to the prehistoric times. Men were believed to be hunters, while women were believed to be gatherers. Men generally did the hunting and women did the gathering. Prehistoric men had the hunting instinct. The men left the family and went out to hunt animals, to feed themselves and their families. Meanwhile, the women gathered plants and other food items needed for the family. The women in the prehistoric times did not require a *"hunting instinct"*, instead, their instinct was to tend to the survival of the children and the home. However, research shows that prehistoric women were just as skilled at hunting and killing game as men were. This goes to show you that women have always been strong and fierce. You will learn throughout history, and even today, that women are able to do whatever they set their minds to do.

Today, men still have the *"hunting instinct."* Men are often in hunting mode for the mate of their choice. Men enjoy what we often call *"the thrill of the chase."* **Thrill of the Chase:** This refers to the excitement that people feel when they are trying hard to get something. Many men find outlets for their hunting instincts in the world today by pursuing and chasing after attainable things in life. They also chase after the woman that catches their eye or piques their interest. Usually, by chasing after her for love, attention, and affection, once they have it, they feel a great sense of value and self-worth. This manifests as a tremendous ego boost and improved confidence in their masculinity.

Many men find the chase to be very exhilarating. They find it exciting to have their egos stroked as often as possible. It's wonderful for them to feel they're the one who is ultimately going to get her attention. This logic may sound foreign to us, but this is exactly how men think. Men love the chase and it can be attributed to their very large egos. Men are intrigued when a woman is not available or accessible to them. Something in their brain tells them that they must get her attention and it is essential to have her in their life. Men are very competitive. When they actually achieve something or acquire something or someone that is deemed impossible or out of their league, you can't tell them anything! Their heads are super inflated.

Research indicates that for many people, *"the pursuit of the chase is more enticing and rewarding than the actual relationship itself."* According to research, men tend to lose interest after the chase. They have the prize!

In order to have a thriving and lasting marriage, it takes work. The husband's continual pursuit of his wife plays a vital role in maintaining love, romance, and connection. Pursuit involves intentional actions and gestures that demonstrate ongoing affection, admiration, and effort to keep the flame of love burning. Before marriage and during the newlywed stage, your husband couldn't get enough of you. He made you feel special. His actions convinced you that he was madly in love with you. He couldn't imagine the thought of not having you in his life. Early in the relationship, your husband pursued you vigorously. Listed below are a few ways your husband likely pursued you during the honeymoon phase of your marriage:

- He told you he loved you every day and multiple times a day.

- He called or texted you every day and multiple times a day.
- He told you that he missed you.
- He planned dates.
- He complimented you regularly.
- He was very affectionate with you.
- He brought flowers or small gifts regularly.
- He walked side-by-side with you.
- He opened doors for you.
- He was very attentive.
- He was extremely mentally and emotionally available.
- He aimed to satisfy you sexually.

I'm sure we can definitely become accustomed to being treated this way by our husbands. Now that our husbands have us, we don't want them to easily forget how they got us. Remember growing up and hearing older people share the lessons and experiences they learned along the way? They were always sharing wisdom with the younger generation. For instance, husbands must remember: *"The same thing it took to get her. It's going to take the same thing to keep her."* That'll preach!

When the wife does not feel pursued in the marriage, she feels alone and undesirable. She feels empty, abandoned, and unfilled. She feels as though she is losing something valuable in her marriage. A husband being in pursuit of his wife is essential for keeping the romance alive in a marriage. A wanted and desired wife is a happy wife. Never stop courting or dating her. We love for our husbands to take us out on fun, exciting and romantic dates. The same dates we went on when we were dating will be fine with us. Even though our husbands won the proverbial prize when they married us, we want them to continue pursuing us, as if they haven't won the prize. They should never get too comfortable and start taking their wives and their marriages for granted. It can potentially end badly for them. It's very simple! I repeat: The same things he did to get you, he needs to do the same things to keep you. As a matter of fact, it wouldn't hurt for him to do more. He should never become complacent, always date his wife, and always make her feel wanted and desirable. Remember, a wife who feels desired is a happy wife.

Continue To Woo Her: Many men feel as if they can stop pursuing their wives after the wedding because *"they have them now,"* right? This is absolutely false. This is a terrible idea. Husbands should continue to woo their wives. They should keep the romance and charm alive, no matter how many years they've been married. They claimed to have had game when they were dating you.

Obviously, it worked because we married them, right? We want our husbands to date us; write us love notes and leave them throughout the house, in our lunch bag, in our daily planner, on our computer or in our briefcase. Continue to treat us like the queens that we are. We already love our husbands but, their responsibility is to focus on making us fall in love with them over and over again. Wooing your wife typically encompasses three actions:

- Allure Your Wife
- Be Attentive
- Spend Time Together

Allure Your Wife. Allure is basically another word for woo, charm, or pursue. When your husband is trying to allure you, he wants to impress you. He wants to get your attention. He wants to prove to you that he loves you and that he realizes that you are a catch. You are worth keeping. You are considered top tier in eyes. According to Hosea 2:14, this was something God did to win back His bride.

> ***Therefore, behold, I will allure her, and bring her into the wilderness, and speak comfortably unto her.***
> ***Hosea 2:14 (KJV)***

In Hosea 2:14, the Bible says, "*Therefore,*" so in light of all of the sin, idolatry, immorality, spiritual adultery, we read the word, "*Therefore*". One could've expected a different response. Particularly a response where judgment was definitely imminent. But listen to what God says. "*Therefore, in light of all of this, I will allure her, and I will bring her into the wilderness and speak tenderly to her.*" Is that not an amazing verse? God's people, deserving God's judgment, and He says, "*In light of your sin against me, here's what I'm going to do. I'm going to allure you. Allure and captivate you with my love. I'm going to pour out my affection on you in such a way that you would be drawn to me. I'm going to allure you. I'm going to bring you into the wilderness.*" In other words, "*I'm going to pull you aside and speak tenderly to you.*" What a Word!

Prayer: God, we thank You and we give You praise. We praise you for your love, for your loving pursuit of us, for your running after us, even when we weren't running after You. God, even when we're disobedient, and run away from You and run to the things of this world, You still pursue us. You give us more opportunities than we deserve to come to You. You love us just that much! Lord, God help us to get in a hurry and run to You. Everything we need, we can find in You. In Jesus' name, Amen.

Be Attentive. One way to show your spouse that you love them is to give them your attention. It is not about being clingy, it's about making a conscious effort to improve the relationship. It's one thing to be in the same room, it's another to be present together. It's all about being thoughtful, patient and kind. It's about listening well and also being an active participant in the conversation. It is very important for both spouses to reveal parts of their inner selves to each other. During the dating stage of your relationship, it is obviously filled with pursuing activities. Your husband was on the hunt to get you. Your husband wanted you to know that he was very interested in you. Undoubtedly, he wanted to spend a considerable amount of his time with you. You had his full attention.

I know we all have a life separate from our spouses. We have work, friends, activities, social clubs, church groups, children, and school, just to name a few. Sometimes, one spouse is so immersed in work that they forget that they have a life beyond it. I'm sure there is nothing worse than having a husband who comes home tired from work and doesn't have time for you. It would make you feel completely unnoticed and ignored. Speaking from a wife's perspective, this behavior would make us very unhappy.

Here are a couple ways you can give your spouse the attention they need and deserve.

- Get off of the phone when your spouse is trying to talk to you.
- Put your phone away and give them your undivided attention.
- Listen to what your spouse has to say.
- Demonstrate how engaged you are in the conversation. You can do this by turning towards your spouse and displaying good eye contact. You

can also use non-verbal cues to indicate that you're listening.

A husband who is pursuing his wife and giving her his undivided attention assures her that he is still in love with her, he is attracted to her, he is interested in her, he cares about her, and that he is totally devoted to her and he is invested in the marriage.

Spend Time Together. I love this quote: *"A man in love is in constant pursuit."* His every action is directed toward what or whom he loves most. Every meaningful marriage or relationship needs time and attention. Time and attention received from our husbands are considered as currency that is deposited into our emotional love banks.

Finding ways to sustain love involves spending time together. It is important to make time for romance daily. This dedicated, uninterrupted time together fosters intimacy, builds trust, and strengthens the emotional connection within the marriage. Love grows and develops over time, but it can quickly fall apart without the proper foundation. Thriving couples build a strong friendship by continuing to date and nurture the marriage.

Don't stop doing the little things you did together when you first started dating. Date nights are a great way to spend time together. If you remember correctly, those were the good ole days. You might have a lot going on in your life; we all do. It's so important to plan regular outings and date nights, and do whatever it takes to make it happen. Your marriage needs it. This means making time together a priority. You must be intentional. Canceling planned date nights are unacceptable. Making time for your spouse and spending quality time with them is important in strengthening connections and forming deeper connections. Song of Solomon 3:1-2 are perfect scriptures for husbands and wives to read. They can follow the example of the bride in Song of Solomon: *"By night on my bed I sought the one I love; I sought him but did not find him. 'I will rise now,' I said, 'and go about the city; in the streets and in the squares I will seek the one I love'"* (Song of Solomon 3:1-2 KJV). To paraphrase, married couples should continue to pursue each other just as you did, back in the day, before you were married.

    A serious lack of quality time in marriages and relationships can chip away at the foundation. It will weaken all connections that have been formed. A couple that doesn't spend a lot of meaningful time together may question whether they truly love one another anymore, or whether the marriage has become more of a roommate situation? How a husband spends his time with his wife can show her that he loves her and values her. It can also show her that he doesn't care about her and that he is taking her for granted. In cases like this, your spouse might feel forgotten and feel like they aren't a priority to you. This then leads to feelings of neglect and resentment. You then start becoming more distant from one another and less likely to share any exciting experiences. As a result, a disconnect and breakdown in the marriage can occur.

Caveat: Eventually, the amount of time couples spend together may decrease, which is also perfectly normal. Having your personal time and space is also vital for a healthy marriage.

Pursue Her Body. I was raised in the Pentecostal Church of God In Christ faith. Premarital sex was absolutely forbidden. I know many of you were probably raised in a similar household that prohibited sex before marriage, as well. According to 1 Corinthians 7:1, it is good for a man not to touch a woman.

> ***Now concerning the things whereof ye wrote unto me: It is good for a man not to touch a woman. Nevertheless, to avoid fornication, let every man have his own wife, and let every woman have her own husband.***
> ***1 Corinthians 7:1-2(KJV)***

Think back to the days when you and your spouse were courting. During the dating phase you both were probably holding hands, kissing, and hugging. As you were engaging in these activities, you noticed that your body had a reaction. Your body began to respond to the physical touch. Undoubtedly, you became very aroused. You are human. (Stay with me. I'm going somewhere with this!) Remember the days when you probably wanted to go further, but you both knew it was wrong? You dreamt of the day when you two could finally be together. You dreamt of the day when you could know one another in the biblical sense. Remember those days? The thought of touching and caressing each other's body was exciting? Your heart was racing profusely. You couldn't wait to explore each other. By exploring, I mean taking the time to look at, feel, and touch every inch of your partner's body. Once you got married, and now you're husband and wife, you finally consummated the marriage and it was magical. I said all of that to say this, don't ever let the fire and passion for each other die. Before marriage, you wanted to sop each other up with a biscuit. However, you knew you couldn't engage in such activities before marriage. Continue to fan the flames of love and passion to ensure a lasting marriage. A husband should continue to pursue his wife's body and tell her all of the things he absolutely loves about her. I love it when my husband pulls me close to him, hugs me and gives me a passionate kiss. He assures me that he finds me attractive and desirable.

Sex Starts Outside of the Bedroom. In order for love, romance, and passion to intensify, the husband must know how to touch his wife's heart before he touches her body. Generally, men don't seem to realize that passion and romance actually start outside the bedroom. Oftentimes, our husbands touch our bodies and expect that we will automatically respond to them. They seem to think we should automatically respond passionately just because they touched us. Typically, that's not how it works. If truth be told, we need a little warming up. Sometimes, we're not quite ready yet. What has he done to set the mood? We want attention and affection outside the bedroom. He can start by preparing the ambiance that sets the mood all throughout the day. For example, he can text you sweet nothings during the day. He can tell you how much he loves you. He can let you know how happy he is to have you as his wife. Be flirtatious and tease each other to build the anticipation of what can be expected when you both get home that night. Trust me, that mood will carry over into the bedroom!

"Let the husband render to his wife the affection due her, and likewise also the wife to her husband."
1 Corinthians 7:3 (NKJV)

Chase her. Chase her even when she's already yours. That's the only way you'll be assured to never lose her.
Anonymous

Marriage is a wonderful journey of love, where two people are evolving together every day. Marriage is work. In order to have a great marriage, you must put in the work. My husband and I have been married for over eight years. I love him and he loves me. I work his nerves sometimes and he works mine occasionally, too. It's okay, this happens in a marriage. It isn't always peaches and cream. You won't find a perfect marriage. Don't be deceived by everything you see on that little blue app. Stay focused on your own marriage and stop comparing your marriage or relationship to others.

My husband and I made a vow to one another before God, July 24, 2015. *"We promised to be each other's wedded spouse, to have and to hold from that day forward, for better, for worse, for richer, for poorer, in sickness and in health, to love and to cherish, till death do us part."* We took our vows very seriously and God willing, we are determined to honor them.

I can honestly say that my husband understands his assignment; to God be the Glory! He is led by God and I'm happy to continue submitting to his leadership. Yes, Elder Brown and I have decided to continue riding through the highs and the lows of life together. We love each other. We're here to stay. We're having fun! With

God on our side, we will make it. Remember, with God on your side, you will, too.

DR. GREEN-BROWN'S
TIDBITS OF WISDOM

It is very important for husbands and wives to love one another and to always invest in their marriage. Marriage is work. Some couples might make it look easy, but trust me, it's not always easy. It takes work. It is doable. You must be willing to put in the work. I say to all married couples: Love each other and don't hesitate to let your spouse know that they are loved and appreciated every day. Whisper sweet nothings in their ear and make them blush! Think of something sweet and romantic to say. If you just can't think of anything, I can assist you. Tell your spouse:

1. I love you.
2. I respect you.
3. We are a team.
4. I will always be by your side.
5. I will always have your back.
6. Your happiness is my happiness.
7. I'll always be your biggest cheerleader.
8. No matter what, let's stay together.

9. You are my happy place.
10. My life is happy because of you.
11. I love everything about you.
12. Every day with you is better than the last.
13. You have my heart.
14. I choose you, all day every day.
15. Our future will get brighter and brighter.
16. I'm happy when you're happy.
17. I love waking up to you every morning.
18. I love falling asleep next to you every night.
19. You make me happy every day.
20. I'm yours.
21. I'm so happy to be married to you.
22. You were worth the wait.
23. There is absolutely nothing I wouldn't do for you.
24. I could search the whole world and never find another person like you.
25. Home is wherever you are.
26. Our best is yet to come.
27. I want to grow old with you.
28. You are worth fighting for.
29. Life is better with you by my side.
30. I thank God every day for you.

Love on each other every day!

ABOUT THE AUTHOR

Dr. Tracie Green-Brown is a Retired Educator, Advocate, Mentor, Servant Leader, Professional Certified Christian Life Coach, Certified Christian Mentor and Published Author.

Dr. Green-Brown is married to the love of her life, Elder Rickey Brown, who found her and made her his wife over 8 years ago. They share 5 amazing children and 2 equally amazing grandchildren.

Dr. Green-Brown holds a:
- Bachelor of Science Degree in Family and Consumer Sciences from Mississippi College
- Master of Science in Education in Guidance and Counseling from Jackson State University
- Master of Arts in Teaching (MAT) in English from Jackson State University
- Education Specialist in Educational Leadership from Arkansas State University
- Doctor of Philosophy in Christian Counseling from New Foundation Theological Seminary

Dr. Green-Brown has real world experience in the field of education, as a high school teacher, for eleven (11) years; and as a professional school counselor for the past seventeen (17) years. With twenty-eight (28) years of experience as an educator, she has developed an unrelenting passion for helping students succeed. This passion has spilled over into other areas of her life.

As a Certified Christian Life Coach, Dr. Green-Brown is very passionate about helping others succeed. Her passion for the work of Christian Life Coaching stems from her own past struggles. Her purpose is to educate, encourage, and empower others to reach their fullest potential, live abundant lives and authentically be the best version of themselves. Dr. Green-Brown believes everyone, if given the proper guidance and tools, can find a path to their own personal success.

Dr. Green-Brown is a two-time published author. Her inaugural book is appropriately titled, *My Story: Surviving the Worst to Get to My Best.* She takes us through her journey of life in an abusive marriage. She tells her story in hopes of empowering women in similar situations to seek help, get out and live their best lives.

Her latest book is a 31-Day Devotional Journal titled, *Surviving the Covid-19 Pandemic: A Guide for Students.* This book is a 31-day processing journal designed to alleviate anxiety and stress for students who were struggling with the new normal due to the Covid-19 Pandemic. This journal provides an opportunity for students to engage in self-reflection and gain a deeper understanding of self.

Since retiring, Dr. Green-Brown spends her days reading, writing, supervising home improvements and enjoying the fruits of her labor!

Contact Dr. Green-Brown

coachtgreenbrown@gmail.com
coachtgreenbrown.com
Facebook: Tracie Green-Brown
Instagram: coachgreenbrown
TikTok: drgreenbrown

Book Description

In *When Husbands Understand Their Assignment: A Wife's Perspective*, Author Dr. Tracie Green-Brown bring readers along as she offers advice and strategies to having a successful marriage. The greatest commandment, found in Mark 12:30, says, *"Thou shalt love the Lord thy God with all thy heart, and with all thy soul, and with all thy mind, and with all thy strength."*

Dr. Green-Brown firmly believes that when a husband truly loves God, he will love his wife correctly. He will know how to love her because he has the Holy Spirit working in him. It is the personal relationship with God that allows him to love his wife as Christ loved the church.

This book affirms a powerful message for every woman; especially for those women who are waiting to be found by their husbands.

Dr. Green-Brown shares personal experiences and suggest specific characteristics to look for in a potential husband. She adamantly encourages woman to wait, watch and pray. Husbands are commissioned by God to be leaders, providers, protectors, and companions. God has placed a tremendous responsibility on their shoulders. For this reason, it is imperative that husbands understand their assignment.

www.ingramcontent.com/pod-product-compliance
Lightning Source LLC
Chambersburg PA
CBHW070648160426
43194CB00009B/1624